W9-BZV-083

On Being Human

On Being Human

Sexual Orientation and the Image of God

C. Norman Kraus

 CASCADE *Books* · Eugene, Oregon

ON BEING HUMAN
Sexual Orientation and the Image of God

Copyright © 2011 C. Norman Kraus. All rights reserved. Except for brief quotations in critical publications or reviews, no part of this book may be reproduced in any manner without prior written permission from the publisher. Write: Permissions, Wipf and Stock Publishers, 199 W. 8th Ave., Suite 3, Eugene, OR 97401.

Cascade Books
A Division of Wipf and Stock Publishers
199 W. 8th Ave., Suite 3
Eugene, OR 97401

www.wipfandstock.com

ISBN 13: 978-1-61097-198-0

Cataloging-in-Publication data:

Kraus, C. Norman (Clyde Norman), 1924–.

On being human : sexual orientation and the image of God / C. Norman Kraus.

xvi + 114 p. ; 23 cm. Includes bibliographical references.

ISBN 13: 978-1-61097-198-0

1. Homosexuality—Religious aspects—Christianity. 2. Homosexuality in the Bible. 3. Sex—Religious aspects—Christianity. 4. Theological anthropology. I. Title.

BT708 K68 2011

Manufactured in the U.S.A.

Contents

Foreword

A Mennonite Response to *On Being Human*

NORMAN KRAUS AND I ARE BOTH OCTOGENARIANS WHO
have seen many changes in the congregations of our church. In
the 1940s we were students in Eastern Mennonite School (now
EMU). He was a college student and I was a high school student.
Our ways soon parted. He pursued theological studies, joined the
faculty of Goshen College, Goshen, Indiana, and served as a missionary scholar to the Mennonite church in Japan. I opted to serve
in Civilian Public Service as a conscientious objector, get married, and, in 1950, accepted the call of Eastern Mennonite Board
of Missions and Charities (now EMM) to serve as a missionary
pastor in Tampa, Florida. In 1961, the Lancaster Mennonite
Conference ordained me to serve as the bishop for its churches
in Florida, Georgia and South Carolina, and in 1975 I began to
serve as an executive for a new Southeast Mennonite Conference.
I've preached many sermons before and since my retirement from
conference work in 1992. At Kraus's invitation, I am sharing a pastoral response to his scholarly thesis.

My first exposure to serious questions about sexuality was
in a workshop sponsored by Dr. Enos Martin, a psychiatrist and
bishop in the Lancaster Mennonite Conference. The workshop
assumed that homosexuality was an evil and that a homosexual's

orientation could be changed. The purpose of the workshop was to advance the use of Alcoholics Anonymous strategies to minister to homosexuals in the congregation.

One of the lecturers at the workshop was a New Testament scholar, Dr. George R. Brunk III. As I remember it, Brunk cautioned us not to take a position on sexual matters based on a simple reading of the English Bible. Brunk explained that students of the original languages do not know the precise meaning of many of the words for sexual behavior used in the Bible since the ancients used euphemisms to keep private matters private, just as we do in our own culture. For instance, "restroom" is a common euphemism which we understand today. But, will anyone know the use of a "restroom" 2,000 years from now? Translators can only guess at the best English words to use when translating Hebrew and Greek euphemisms. Brunk suggested that the creation story is the safest, wisest place to begin the study of sexuality in the Bible.

With skills sharpened by decades of biblical study and teaching, observation of cultures from a missionary's perspective, and after lifelong reflection, C. Norman Kraus offers a treatise for study by the whole church. Simply put, Kraus presents a case for the view that sexual orientation is an essential part of being human; that a human is not responsible for his or her sexual orientation; that homosexual identity is no more perverse than heterosexual identity, and guidelines for both homo-erotic and hetero-erotic behaviors should be identical.

While Kraus is not gay, it is obvious that he feels for those who have come out of the closet and suffered because of it. But he is not only motivated by empathy for them, so why does he write on their behalf? His words reveal what moved him. He believes that "how the church deals with sexual variants within its fellowship is a test of its authenticity as the body of Christ." To lack authenticity is to lack credibility and effectiveness. As churchman and missionary, Kraus is concerned for any church that wants to be missional and win the lost, only to find its saving message weakened and made less believable by excluding gay believers.

Kraus's essay is both an invitation and a challenge. He invites pastors and teachers to quit judging and excluding. He challenges churches to look through the powerful lens of their own mission statements to examine how the treatment of sexual variants robs their witness of authenticity, authority, and effectiveness. I concur with Kraus that if the challenge is rejected, those who need Jesus may not believe him, the Holy Spirit will be grieved, the church's growth as a community of grace, joy, and peace will be slowed, and the flow of healing and hope from the church to the world will be restricted. This sounds harsh, but it must be said.

An Uneasy Church

Many denominations have been asked to soften their stance against homosexuality, but the pleas go unheeded. Unease mounts when a growing number of non-gay believers urge their denomination to allow congregations to welcome gays and lesbians. Most Christians would agree with the Mennonite mission statement that "God calls us to be followers of Jesus Christ and, by the power of the Holy Spirit, to grow as communities of grace, joy and peace, so that God's healing and hope flow through us to the world." But most congregations also are generally uneasy if they have no standards to follow, and in their anxiety and desire to follow Christ they search for concrete directives and rules.

Seeking such directives in July of 1995, a majority of a newly formed Mennonite Church USA approved *A Confession of Faith from an Anabaptist Perspective*. But the *Confession* has become virtually a *creedal* standard and Levitical in nature as it relates to homosexuality. Some Mennonite conferences have dismissed congregations that accepted believing gay persons into their fellowship. Individuals and churches that are expelled are often painfully isolated and frustrated when they cannot use their gifts in service to the church.

Church leaders seem to fear that some congregations and perhaps whole conferences will split away from the denomination and add yet more division to an already severely divided Anabaptist movement. Like other firm-minded, anti-gay denominations they fear that their denomination will yield to cultural pressure and welcome gays and lesbians, especially those in committed partnerships. The sincerity of the various elements within the church ought not to be questioned, but granted that these churches are using the limited knowledge they have, should we not be open to the new data about sexuality and cultural changes that define our contemporary situation? Kraus argues that the church's knowledge needs to be expanded.

A Lesson in Theology

In his essay Kraus cites the work of scientists who have researched the sources of sexual orientation, and he notes that they disagree on the definition of orientation, its source, and how to interpret the data collected by the various schools of scientific thought. These disagreements among scientists complicate matters for the church and are a source of confusion.

But Kraus does not rely on scientific data to defend his thesis. It is interesting to me that as a theologian he begins as Brunk had suggested earlier—at the beginning. Theologians may begin their studies at the creation or the Fall, but Kraus would have them begin with the Creator's personal being as the analogue of the divine image in humanity. He begins with the Genesis account of creation and the essential being of God who pronounced humankind "in our image." This personal God of the beginning revealed in the Bible comes later to be understood as the Tri-unity of Father, Son, and Holy Spirit. In the mystery of this personal-social essence the human race was created as social beings in the hope they would be an exhibit of the divine image.

My Bahia Vista Sermon

I was impressed with this social framing of the creation of humankind years ago when I was preparing a sermon for the Bahia Vista Mennonite Church in Florida. Using the simple tool provided by *Strong's Exhaustive Concordance* I learned that the first word used for God in the Hebrew Bible is "Elohim." Elohim is a plural noun that is found more than 2,500 times in the Hebrew Scriptures. Most often it is used in relation to the God of Israel, but it is also used of the plural gods of other nations. Perhaps the word "Elohim" originated in the polytheistic world in which Abraham was born.

The plural name of God is supported by the plural pronouns in Genesis 1:26–27: God said, "Let *us* make man in *our* image, in *our* likeness, and let them rule . . ." The plural pronouns affirm that the God of the beginning is a community of equals. Though the plural name for God was likely borrowed from a polytheistic past, the Old Testament insists that Israel's Elohim was superior to the elohim of Israel's neighbors. The superiority of Israel's Elohim is in a unity so unique that it may be described as being one. At Mount Sinai the voice of God instructed the people, "Hear, O Israel, Jehovah our Elohim is one Jehovah" (Deut 6:4). That is still the confession of all Israelis who keep their covenant with God. Jesus affirmed it. Yet, Jesus was rejected because he made himself equal with God. In my sermon in 2002, I said that Jesus came to restore the Elohim of the beginning.

While the word "Trinity" is not found in the Bible, yet the presence of God as social being is pervasive in the New Testament. Near the beginning of Jesus' ministry, John baptized him at the Jordan River. The *Spirit* descended on *Jesus* in the form of a dove and *a voice* announced from heaven, "this is my Son, whom I love; with him I am well pleased." In the last hours of his ministry, Jesus prayed that his disciples would be one as he and the Father are one so that the world would believe that God had sent him.

Several years after preaching the above sermon, I learned that the Greek Fathers described this social aspect of the Trinity as a *perochoresis*, which being interpreted means a dance in which one partner leads, and the other(s) follow. In the dance of the trinitarian Deity, the lead role is passed around among the three equal partners with perfect grace, harmony, joy, and mutual respect. In a theological sense, there is a perfect community in the true God. In contrast the gods of Israel's neighbors were sometimes depicted as being selfish, jealous, and at odds.

In the beginning, the dancing equals created the earth and out of its dust formed a pair of innocent humans in their divine image. Their descendants were meant to be a community that freely chose to live as one in world-wide *shalom*. When the divine image was marred by sin, God so loved the world that he sent his only Son, Jesus, to save the people from their sins, call them to live in peace, and, invite them to join in the eternal dance of the triune God.

This is the gospel we preach. But the prayer of Jesus in John 17 implies that the church's preaching will be believed worldwide only when the church is in the image of the biblical Elohim. Then the church's witness will be powerfully authentic, credible, and effective.

The Art of Deconstruction-Reconstruction

St. Augustine, (354–430 A.D.), a teacher of the early church, made a sharp distinction between humanity as created, and sinful humanity as fallen. He identified heterosexuality as God's intent, and considered all same-sex erotic urges to be moral flaws caused by the sin of the first human parents. Kraus argues that Augustine's view of sexuality weakens the church today, and now is the time for the evangelical church to deconstruct the Augustinian theological traditions and to reconstruct a theology that allows the Bible to speak its authentic word of grace. He declares that "Indeed, this work of de-constructing-reconstructing in the spirit of Christ is precisely the work of the Holy Spirit in the church."

Deconstruction and reconstruction were new words to me, but the concept was easily grasped. The earthquake and voice of thunder at Mount Sinai in the wilderness signaled an end to the era of salvation through simple patriarchal faith and introduced salvation through obedience to the law. Deconstruction and reconstruction happened when Jesus taught, "You have heard that it has been said, but I say unto you . . ." It happened at the Jerusalem Conference when they wrote, "it seemed good to the Holy Spirit and to us to lay on you no greater burden." It happened in 1525 when Grebel, Manz, and Blaurock baptized each other as adults in defiance of ecclesiastical and state law and initiated the believer's church.

I understand the phenomena because I lived through it. Anyone who doubts that changes took place in the 1960s should ask an octogenarian. In the 1960s Mennonite congregations quietly followed the Spirit in deconstructing their interpretation of 1 Corinthians 11 and reconstructing it to allow women members to cut their hair, and to pray and teach in the church with uncovered heads. The deconstruction of other words on women's role was more painful and given more debate. That women should remain silent in the churches and be in submission "as the Law also says" (1 Cor 14:34) was eventually altered to allow women to speak in churches and be ordained for senior pastoral leadership. Matthew 19:3–12 and related scriptures were reconstructed to welcome divorced and remarried persons as members of the congregation. The process of deconstruction-reconstruction is not finished for the world is still changing. The Holy Spirit is still teaching, and the church is still learning.

While the agencies of Mennonite Church USA seem to be functioning effectively in mission, mutual aid, and service networks, stripped of these agencies, the church appears weak and confused. Most Mennonites, like other Christians, have failed to live up to their calling. They have not done the work needed to de-construct the teachings and fears that cause them to distort and spurn the evidence of God's grace toward believing homosexuals. They justify division, not recognizing it as the grievous sin it is. They have not reconstructed a church that welcomes all who believe.

But there is hope. When the late George R. Brunk II, who was a scholar, tent evangelist, Dean of Eastern Mennonite Seminary, and staunch defender of the faith, learned that one of his grandsons was gay, grandfather and grandson became estranged for many years. In the last years of his life, however, grandfather Brunk initiated a conversation with his grandson. The two honored the agreement not to disclose what transpired between them. But when questioned later, the elder Brunk simply said, "We should have talked a long time ago." It may be presumed that the grandfather listened as well as talked.

Kraus's essay offers a new opportunity to the church. There may be a gracious intervention, an outpouring of the Holy Spirit that exalts Jesus Christ and saves the church and the world. It behooves all evangelical leaders, every faithful pastor, teacher, and evangelist, and everyone concerned for the authenticity of the church's message to study Kraus's thesis. No pope or creed can impose unity. *A unifying word for these times must be spoken by the Holy Spirit in the churches through consistent reading, interpretation, and application of Holy Writ, and more, by faithfulness to the Gospel of grace that saves us, and which we preach.*

—Martin Lehman
Goshen, Indiana

Author's Preface

THIS SMALL VOLUME IS INTENDED AS A TEACHING RE-
source for use in study groups. Its perspective is didactic, not polemic. It invites analysis and dialogue not argument. It attempts
to explain how and why historical orthodox tradition in the West
has been and remains so opposed to all same-sex erotic expressions, and examines the theological justification for this position.
It attempts to clarify terminology and concepts, to show how new
socio-biological information affects the discussion, and to present theological options to traditional interpretations. It argues
that the church has followed traditional cultural patterns more
assiduously than it has explored the theological implications of
the historicity of the biblical message.

The authors have not attempted to provide a balanced pro
and con to the knotty cultural and scientific questions that sur-
round the issue. While all of the authors would approve a uni-
form policy of inclusion in the church for everyone regardless of
sexual orientation, it is not our intention to counter all biblical
and ethical arguments against the inclusion of gays and lesbians.
We are convinced that in the present stage of partial ignorance
there are historical, biblical, and ethical grounds for including all
orientations—straight, gay, lesbian, bisexual, and transgendered
(SGLBT)—in a continuing discerning dialogue. The pivotal
question for church membership is not one's sexual orientation,
but what it means to be a follower of Christ.

Four friends have joined me in reflecting on the subject—a retired Mennonite bishop, a pastor of an urban congregation near Washington, DC, a New Testament professor teaching at Associated Mennonite Biblical Seminary, and a theologian and senior editor of the *Christian Century*. I have asked them to make brief complementing responses that can help to foster further dialogue. Their participation in the project does not indicate their full acceptance of my initial essay. For that I alone am responsible.

Having read their responses in the preparation of this manuscript for publication I am tempted to suggest to the readers that they not only read the Foreword, but also Part 2 before they read my presentation. The clarity and personal involvement with which they engage the subject certainly illuminates the more expository and analytical approach of my original text.

—C. Norman Kraus

PART 1

A THEOLOGICAL PERSPECTIVE

Introduction

HOW THE CHURCH DEALS WITH HOMOSEXUALITY IS A theologically based ethical question, not merely a matter of moral propriety based on cultural and political aversion and literal proof-texting. The church's challenge is to reflect the authentic human image of God as a community under God's authority. Thus the social issue of how the church deals with the inclusion or exclusion of minority sexual variants becomes a test of its authenticity as the body of Christ—the New Testament image it claims to represent in the world.

Many of the social and religious mores and sexual disciplines of modern conservative Protestants and Roman Catholics are based on and reference cultural-religious concepts of human nature and relationships that they in fact no longer consistently follow. One has only to compare Islamic sharia to see how far from traditional concepts and patterns of reasoning even conservative evangelical Christianity has come. The Islamic definition of humanity as a natural hierarchy of sexual relationships dominated by physical sexual anatomy is quite similar to the assumptions of ancient and medieval Christian cultures. And the revealed word of Allah is buttressed by and reinforces what Muslims understand to be the "natural order."[1] Traditional societies, such as exist in many African nations, continue to read Christian Scriptures through this cultural lens. Western conservative Protestant

1 Khouj, *Islam*, 149ff.

3

polemics for traditional sexual disciplines references this social paradigm selectively to suit their argument.

From both theological and empirical perspectives, sexual orientation (whether hetero or homo) is an essential aspect of human identity. It is an original, seminal reality in personal identity for which the individual is not responsible. Theologically speaking it is part of the created order. Empirically it is a physically based psychological reality with genetic, prenatal conditioning, and cultural-personal roots. It is the personal disposition that determines the direction in which those sexual attractions, affections, and desires that develop in puberty as sexual self-consciousness manifest themselves, whether toward the opposite sex, the same sex, or some combination of the two, and should not be laden with moral shame and stigma. Sexual identity, or what might be labeled ontological orientation in contrast to situational orientation, should not be labeled sinful or morally perverse, and same-sex inclination is no more morally perverse than heterosexual erotic urges. Thus I argue that moral guidelines for homoerotic attractions and sexual behavior should follow the same pattern as for heterosexual sexual fulfillment.

The social regulation of physical sexual intimacy needs to be formulated within this more broadly defined concept of human sexuality, which frames our volitional, hence moral, decisions and actions. Sexual immorality should not be automatically attached to biologically conditioned physical reflexes/attractions, but to the moral character of personal-social and spiritual relationship. Personal character that reflects the image of God in social relationships is the authenticating mark of moral behavior. Disrespect, violence, rape, abuse, narcissistic self-indulgence, abuse, and violence are always sin against the image of God regardless of the orientation of the actors. Acts of mutual affirmation, respect, and affection that enhance the image are always moral.

The moral dimension of sexuality speaks to how the attractions and desires of all sexual groups are regulated for the common good of society. God's will for the human family is defined in the Bible as *shalom*, which is a human reflection of the trinitarian image of God; and while the inherent spiritual and social meaning of *shalom* does not change, its cultural shape and assumptions do change. At this point, cultural definitions of gender identity and roles enter the picture. Such cultural differences across both temporal and geographical boundaries have always called for adaptation or contextualization of the ancient vision of the image of God in order to maintain the original integrity of transcultural biblical values. Today scientific research has altered traditional cultural outlooks, and the contemporary church must continually adapt its moral and religious guidelines to authentically conserve the biblical vision of *shalom*.

Since sexual self-identity and human self-consciousness are so undivided and inseparable, we must approach the matter of sexual identity with caution and reverence, not suspicion and stigma. Psychologically speaking, demands for change in homosexually oriented individuals should be approached with empathetic deliberation. Indeed, in order to grasp the nature of the problem it may help exclusively heterosexually oriented individuals to imagine themselves being pressured to change their straight orientation or to refrain from sexual behavior unless with same-sex partners. Pressures for change, of course, are placed upon the minority for both biological and social reasons since the biological end of sexuality is clearly the preservation of the human species. But when preservation of the race is not endangered, homosexual preferences and behavior need not be treated as a moral taboo. From the church's perspective homosexual behavior should be socially regulated as a minority variant for the fulfillment of God's image of *shalom* in the human family.

I have not attempted to spell out the finer casuistic ethical issues and personal judgments that will need to be made in individual cases of discernment and membership that confront congregations. These must be made in the face-to-face context of the worshipping community. What I have tried to do is to disabuse our minds of the cultural and theological definitions, presuppositions, and categories that have so far hindered the process of dialogical discernment. Far too often biblical and theological texts have been used as defensive weapons to protect our biases and justify our fears. They have been used in a power play to stop dialogue and discernment rather than to open intelligent, questing debate. If in this small volume I have been able to present an alternative theological approach—an approach I deeply believe in—that will foster the dialogue, I will be satisfied.

1

The "Orientation" Debate

IN SPITE OF THE ENORMOUS AMOUNT OF RESEARCH AND discussion much of our confusion in discussing the moral status of homosexual behavior still stems from semantic ambiguity in classifying sexual identity and preferences. What precisely is sexual *orientation* in humans? Is it more than an emotional affection, attraction, or desire triggered by social relationships? Is it an innate predisposition or sexual self-identity? Is it simply part of our mammalian instinct? If so, does it have a distinctly human personal significance? And how are identity and orientation related? For example, the statement of the Student Counseling Center of the University of Texas blends the two concepts and defines "sexual identity" as primarily a social and biological identity while defining orientation as emotional and/ or physical attraction, adding that orientation is "an integral part of sexual identity."[1] What is the source, and what are the moral genus and implications of sexual self-identity?

The word "orientation" itself has different shades of meaning. For example, first time students arrive early on campus for

1. It continues, "A person's sexual orientation can be heterosexual, homosexual, bisexual, or questioning. All of these sexual orientations are considered to be normal by all prominent mental health organizations, such as the American Psychiatric Association and the American Psychological Association." http://www.utdallas.edu/counseling/selfhelp/sexual-identity.html.

orientation, that is, introduction and adjustment to their new situation. In psychology it is used metaphorically to describe inclinations or preferences, that is, the direction in which one is inclined. The thesaurus lists a host of synonyms: attraction, preference, predilection, proclivity, inclination, predisposition, penchant, and bent. Judging from these synonyms the concrete circumstance that provides the metaphorical meaning is *location* or *direction*, which obviously can be parsed in the direction of either attraction or self-identity.

The nature of sexual orientation itself is debated in medical, psychological, and sociological circles. To be sexually oriented would seem to indicate a sexual self-identity—a location and direction in which one is facing. Its empirical status as innate or acquired attraction is not agreed upon. The American Psychiatric Association (APA), the American Psychological Association, and the National Association of Social Workers consider it an innate psycho-biological identity. In a brief to the Supreme Court of California they testified that "sexual orientation is integrally linked to the intimate personal relationships that human beings form with others to meet their deeply felt needs for love, attachment, and intimacy. In addition to sexual behavior, these bonds encompass nonsexual physical affection between partners, shared goals and values, mutual support, and ongoing commitment."[2] Thus they consider same-sex orientation a normal variant on the human sexual identity continuum, not a mental or physical illness to be diagnosed and treated. Accordingly gays and lesbians, bisexuals, and transsexuals should be accommodated as a normal minority in human society.

But same-sex orientation is also understood by some as simply a psychological preference, attraction, and even an appetite. Those associated with the National Association for Research and Therapy of Homosexuality (NARTH) continue to consider it a medical disorder as the word "therapy" in their name indicates.

2. Case No. SS 147999, "In Remarriage Cases Judicial Council Coordination Proceeding No.4365."

They identify sexual orientation as an *attraction* and assume that it can and should be volitionally converted to conform to heterosexual norms. It is understandable, although questionable, that it would be classified with other appetitive urges since we experience the sex drive as a strong emotional compulsion or urge. Thus those who think of orientation as an attraction—even though a very deep-seated, compulsive attraction—assume that it is amenable to volitional control and change.

The question, then, is whether orientation indicates a constitutive sexual identity that is indivisible from ones self-identity as a human being or whether it is a more incidental acquired sexual attraction or desire, which although conditioned by prenatal influences is a response triggered by random cultural and social stimuli. Both science and religion have wrestled with these questions, and neither has come to an answer with which all agree. In the last two decades the scientific community has made strides in research, and the APA and NARTH have moved nearer to agreement on issues that are amenable to empirical investigation, but they continue to disagree on the morally normative implications of other-than-heterosexual orientations.

The Bible refers to what we call self-identity as the "image of God" and clearly includes sexuality in this image. But how is this sexuality to be understood? Is it essentially a biological phenomenon manifested in the physical anatomy of male and female? Does the original image spoken of in Genesis 1:28–29 refer to physical sexual complementarities of male and female and to be equated with the heterosexual orientation of individuals, as Robert Gagnon and others hold?[3] Are we to understand it in terms of physical coitus (sex) and child bearing? Or is it a social and spiritual image of God reflected in the personal ordering of human society?

How we understand this sexual metaphor of the image of God is crucial to the church's self-understanding as the people of God called to reflect God's image. It is my contention that sexuality

3. Gagnon, *The Bible and Homosexual Practice*.

conditions the whole gamut of human relations, and thus is a social phenomenon. It affects all the dimensions of our personal being, not least our spirituality. It conditions our affectional preferences, our physical choices, and our rational orientation.

While the normative concern is ultimately theological, and empirical research alone cannot resolve normative issues, the church's moral evaluation of sexual orientation must consider whether it is simply an acquired attraction or an inherent aspect in core human identity; and disagreement among empirical researchers complicates the question of sexual orientation's normative status for the church.

The Biblical Problem

Complicating our task is the hermeneutical question of comparing ancient and modern scientific conceptions of sexuality. Awareness of same-sex attraction and behavior in the Bible is at least as ancient as the pre-diluvian corruption described in Genesis. The present-day concept of same-sex *orientation*, on the other hand, is a relatively recent psychological classification to accommodate the increasing evidence from empirical research. Its precise meaning and significance for social management is still being sorted out. It represents new data that scientific research is still refining, data simply not available until recent decades. Implicit is the question of whether same-sex attraction is a mental disorder, a moral perversion, a physical disability, or yet a different human phenomenon. In short, same-sex orientation is an empirical designation whose theological and moral significance is still in exploration and debate.[4]

4. Hendrik Hart in his foreword to Pim Pronk's *Against Nature* notes that "Orientation is, as such, not the same as sex or gender. But it affects both, since homosexuals often do not play a sexually reproductive role and sometimes do accept gender traits not traditionally associated with their sex" (p. vii). Pronk's detailed analysis is quite helpful in understanding the new insights that modern empirical research has contributed to our conceptualization of deviant orientations.

As a whole, biblical regulations promoted a high standard of sexual responsibility, based on the understandings of ancient Hebrew culture. Sexual mores regulated the propagation of the hierarchical, sometimes polygamous, family system to promote social well-being, although they were not framed as consequential social rules. The proscriptions of the Holiness Code in Leviticus (Lev 17–26) are imposed as a reflection of God's nature and character (holiness), which was the moral sanction for all social regulations (righteousness) in Israel. In anthropological terms, the prohibitions are usually stated as taboos. They forbid or require certain behaviors simply as divine fiat representing God's essential character. No rational, social, or personal explanations for the regulations are offered. The rationale for prohibitions is simply that they are out of character with and an "abomination" to Yahweh, Israel's God.

While the Bible is clearly concerned with both the social welfare and the propagation of the human family, yet we dare not forget that Yahweh's will and character were perceived and elucidated in anthropological terms *directly related to the ancient cultural, social, and physical understandings.* As these understandings changed, behaviors and social practices associated with them changed, and biblical interpretation has undergone continuous modification and adaptation in the centuries since to maintain its authentic relevance. Especially in the last two centuries our cultural outlook has been so altered by scientific advance and revolutionary political and social developments that our biological and psychological understanding of sexual orientation and its moral regulation requires this same kind of analysis and adaptation. But contemporary contextualization of biblical texts has too often not taken into account the implications of modern demographics, or the most current empirical findings that bear on earlier moral taboos reflected in the texts.

But if we assume, as I do, that God's word to the ancients was framed in the terms and vocabulary of their worldviews and cultural perceptions, we must take seriously the new information that modern research has uncovered when applying those words to our modern situation. To the ancients, for example, to speak of homosexual behavior as "unnatural" implied weird, perverse, or immoral; not simply behavior linked to a statistically calculable genetic variant. It suggested that the subject was defective, something less than human; not to be classified as "normal minority" variation and to be accommodated in human society under the same moral guidelines as the majority of heterosexuals. Of course, if one begins with the hermeneutical presumption that the biblical proscriptions are the direct transcultural dictates of God, or with the definitional assumption that same-sex affective expression cannot be an act of *agape*, such a line of reasoning is beside the point.

And if deviant physical and psychological variations are considered to be moral perversions caused by the inherent sinfulness of humankind, as St. Augustine taught in the fifth century, they must be explicitly classified as a moral deficit, not to be dealt with by therapy, but as profound spiritual temptation and sin. The church must then condemn orientation—both attraction and behavior—as a sinful deviation, and religious counselors should discourage illicit urges and attractions that inflame and incite to "practice" in favor of behaviors acceptable to majority opinion and practice. But is this fifth-century interpretation the final dogmatic biblical interpretation as the Roman Catholic and evangelical Protestant positions suggest?

The Cultural Lag

In spite of major cultural changes caused by scientific outlook, technological advance, and demographic development, political and cultural mores change slowly, and attitudes and legal statutes have remained practically static for the greater part of the twentieth century. Conservative Christians and the political right continue to insist that the clinical "normalization" of homosexual orientation is a secularist conclusion not based strictly on actual scientific evidence and which contradicts the Bible's view of homosexuality. Homophobia and the social disgust factor remain strong, which leads many to keep their orientation closeted, and politicians are loath to recognize the legal legitimacy of same-sex partnering. Most churches have tended to follow the lead of the political and civil community, and those that endorse partnering justify it on the ground of individual rights. Little or no effort has been made to offer a theological rationale. Until recently the United States Army has resolved the issue with an official policy of "Don't ask, don't tell" [your sexual orientation] for its recruits, but it has been hard pressed to justify the constitutionality of this position and is currently in the process of changing its policy.

Traditional Christian religious groups continue to insist that homosexuality is the result of human sinfulness; that the attraction must, at best, be viewed as temptation and that expressing homosexual desire in behavior is an immoral perversion. Some political and religious right-wing conservatives still maintain that there is only one sexual "orientation," namely, heterosexual; and that same-sex affection and sexual intimacy between same-sex partners is unnatural and immoral. It cannot in any legitimate sense be called "love."

Less culturally conservative believers have recognized that various orientations are a biological reality and have tried to distinguish between orientation as physical attraction and behavior ("practice" or "lifestyle"). They agree that sexual orientation is not chosen and is thus nonmoral. But sexual behavior is chosen and thus open to moral evaluation; and on the presumption that genital intimacy between same-sex partners is unnatural and forbidden, they deem the attraction itself to be morally tainted. Since the act of physical intimacy is sinful in itself, the attraction (orientation) must be dealt with as a temptation, just as pedophilia or other immoral and criminal attractions.

Much of the negative reaction to modern developments, which stirs the cultural anxiety of right-wing evangelicals, stems from the assumption that the cultural changes of the last two centuries are due simply to "godless secularism and communism." Change is read as infidelity to the gospel; but change from what? Are all the cultural and ethical developments from the second century CE onwards to be read as moral and religious degeneration? Is an authentic Christianity in the modern era ineluctably linked to accepting the notions of ancient science? And must *Christian* morality be framed in the terms of ancient conceptions of society and the universe? Are there no core values and beliefs that emerge from the *ancient* story of Jesus that can be expressed in modern form? If so, how do we adapt those core convictions, values, and practices in order to preserve them in modern culture? These are the theological questions that we need to ask. And specifically in the case of sexual orientation we must ask how scientific and cultural changes in gender identification and roles impact our moral evaluation of social practice.

The church's initial response, as might be expected from an institution that values ancient norms and seeks to preserve the moral values of the past, has been to conserve traditional sexual morality. This is understandable and perhaps partially justified; but as we move ahead we must come to terms with the theological meaning of the new empirical data and its moral implications in our ongoing contextualization of biblical norms.

As a churchman and theologian I am not qualified to speak authoritatively to the scientific dispute, but the final resolution of the issues for ethical evaluation and social action is not purely empirical. It requires examination of assumptions and analysis based on biblical, philosophical, theological, and ethical considerations. However, while the final determinant for the church is theological, theology must consider the latest empirical research to maintain the contextual integrity of the Bible's teaching. The Bible has valid authority for today only when its meaning for its initial audience is properly understood and correct analogies to our contemporary culture are discerned.

2

Sex, Sexuality, and Changing Culture

THE CLINICAL CONCEPT OF SEXUAL *ORIENTATION* IS OF relatively recent origin, and many people in the religious community may not be aware of the significance of the term. In fact, some argue that ancient attitudes and reactions are quite parallel to the modern. But as Michael Foucault points out, sexual deviation became "a psychological, psychiatric, medical category" from the late nineteenth century on. What was earlier identified with the "act" of sodomy became an "orientation" (a "quality of sexual sensibility") when it was classified as a "contrary sexual sensation" by the German neurologist Carl Westphal in 1870. Foucault comments, "The sodomite had been a temporary aberration; the homosexual was now a species."[1]

The scientific discoveries of genetic and chromosomal evidence, which substantiate the concept of sexual orientation, are even more recent. These researches indicate that there is a physiological continuum of sexual identity, and strictly heterosexual and homosexual genotypes are the extreme ends of this continuum. In between there are a variety of chromosomal combinations that determine the characteristics of physiological anatomy and condition gender identity. As Ruth Hubbard argues

1. Foucault, *The History of Sexuality,* vol. 1, 43.

in *Exploding the Gene Myth* (1993), such discoveries do not indicate that an individual's personality and moral character are physically determined, but the new information has a definite bearing on definitions and moral evaluations.

The clinical conceptualization of sexual orientation was developed in the twentieth-century scientific community as a diagnostic tool to aid in the treatment of psychological and social disorders. It was not intended as a moral or theological classification, but the unintended consequence of its implications has changed the lines of analysis and debate. Before we begin to examine these consequences, however, we need to try to understand the historical perimeters of the cultural development that has given rise to them.

While human cultures and civilizations embody and express similar personal and social values, they do so quite differently. For example, in the ancient Near East and Western cultures permanence was expressed by designing massive stone buildings that defy the erosion of time. By contrast in Japan permanence is joined with renewal in the construction of the Grand Shrine of Amaterasu at Ise by a complete exact rebuilding of the bamboo structure each generation. This variety of expression is to be found not only geographically, but over the sweep of history; and indeed, ancient or traditional culture is not simply a historically past phenomenon. "Ancient" civilization/culture differs significantly from modern, but it is not so long ago or so very far away! It still exists in many geographical pockets of the global world and in many psychological pockets of social relationships even in the "modern" world. Aspects of the old remain in struggle with the new causing what James Davidson Hunter called "culture wars" in his 1992 book, *Culture Wars: The Struggle to Define America.* Yet in Western Europe and large portions of the Americas a genuinely modern culture has evolved in contrast to "premodern" civilization. And in vast areas of Asia and Africa where the ancient still dominates, the modern is only now rapidly becoming the new cultural yardstick.

The church has been quite cautious in accepting the cultural developments of the last 500 years that have created the modern phenomenon. Indeed, the underlying assumption of the religious and politically right wing is that they represent decadence and degeneracy, especially in the area of sexual behavior. While it cannot automatically be assumed that this change in secular philosophy and science is progress, neither dare it all be attributed to the devil. What we must keep in mind, as Phyllis Tickle reminds us in *The Great Emergence*, is that the medieval religious culture of the sixteenth century, to which modernity is contrasted, was just as much of a change from primitive Christianity as the modern (and postmodern) is from the medieval. When the term post-*Christian* was introduced some decades ago, we had to more precisely define it as post-*Christendom*, that is, post half-a-millennium of Western culture known as Christendom. Social analysts were noting that major shifts have taken place in the social-political paradigm, which have affected our values and way of life. But that did not necessarily mean that basic values stemming from New Testament Christianity were passé; rather that new applications were needed to give them authentic relevance to the developing Western culture.

I would argue that it is precisely the work of Christians in society (the church as a social community, not political institution) to help define and promote what "emerges" in the developing culture. In common theological parlance this is often called presenting a "*kingdom* alternative" to both the left- and right-wing political ideologies. But it should not be understood as a power option. Following the nonviolent example of Christ the followers of Jesus are called to spell out the pragmatic implications of love toward those we instinctively fear—those unlike us: the homeless, illegal immigrants, Blacks/Whites, sexually diverse, Muslims, Mexicans, derelicts, and such.

Modern "Secularity"

"Modern," and now "postmodern," has become the label for classifying the major cultural changes that have occurred since the medieval and ancient civilizations. Basic to the social and political development of the past three centuries is a fundamental change in what philosophers call "epistemology"—how we know what we are so sure we know. Of course, we still use our intellect and reason, but "facts"—that is, the actualities of our observable existence—have become basic to our concept of knowledge rather than rationalization based on traditional wisdom. When scientific research contradicts traditional authorities or earlier less precise empirical results, we give credence to the new findings. The heart of empirical scientific research is to discover *what actually is*. Our microscopes, telescopes, and test tubes, our endless biological, botanical, zoological, sociological, psychological, astrological researches are all very much a part of what we identify as the modern quest for knowledge. They are all part of understanding our world and ourselves as we believe God has made us. Deductive logic, which gave philosophers of the medieval period huge room for speculation, has been anchored firmly to inductive scientific observation.

Sometimes we discover "facts" that challenge the accuracy of earlier conceptions upon which we have based social opinions and practices. Some such conception may even be found in the Bible. For example, that the sun rises over a flat earth, that epilepsy is caused by exposure to the moon, and that diseases are caused by spirits inhabiting human bodies. Other examples of scientific findings that have altered our understanding of what it means to be human are that species are not fixed and unalterable that space and time are relative to each other that women are not intellectually and spiritually inferior to men, and that sexual variations have a genetic base and exist along a chromosomal continuum from female to male (XX–XY).

All these modern discoveries have implications for inherited religious beliefs and moral convictions. For example, when diseases and physical deviances are dissociated from evil spirits, they fall into the nonmoral category and are treated clinically rather than religiously. When research uncovers the genetic facts of species development (biological evolution), it changes our understanding of how God has created the world we live in. (Note, not *whether* God created, but *how*.) This is the process that has been transpiring slowly over the millennia, but it has expanded exponentially over the past century causing much cultural uncertainty and anxiety for many. And it is precisely this *modern* empirical perspective altering our understanding of the "facts" that is at the root of Western society's modifications of sexual morality.

This secularizing process began already with the Reformation in the sixteenth century and has altered the way in which we view ourselves and our universe. It has caused us to look at ourselves and our social relationships quite differently from the medieval societal patterns. It has prompted recognition of concepts of individual worth and social equality that totally rule out earlier moral norms that permitted slavery and prostitution. It has affirmed and accentuated personal relationships that have changed the standards of family life and conceptions of abuse. It has emphasized rights to privacy and self-determination that have changed women's role in the sexual relationship. And in the larger society it is the basis for political democracy and individual rights.

I mention these positive characteristics of modern secularity in order to point out that not all the changes in moral and religious thinking that characterize modernity are marks of infidelity to biblical convictions and moral values. Indeed, quite a number of them can be traced back to the original example and teaching of Jesus himself. For example, concepts like equality before God, which have given rise to political democracy and individualism, rest on the twin foundations of ancient Greek philosophy and

Jesus' teaching about God's care for the "least of these." Human dignity for Blacks and the outlawing of slavery along with the recognition of women's equality and children's rights in society stem directly from Jesus. Concepts of privacy—which have become important in judicial decisions regulating social morality—are implied in the recognition of personal worth. And it should be pointed out that it is precisely these changes in the evaluation and worth of human individuals that underlie the challenges to the traditional regulation of sexual morality.

Secularism and relativism are the shadow side of the secularization of Western culture, and have led some to agnosticism and moral skepticism. But we should not throw out the modern baby of secularity with the bathwater of secularism and moral degeneration. A deep respect for the profound theocentric insight of biblical faith—a faith that is rooted in the secularity of historical development—requires the church to take the modern discoveries of science quite seriously as it offers cultural course corrections to society's ever-changing worldview. We must never forget that Jesus himself is a secular historical figure living in late antiquity. He is not merely a religious icon or theological concept. That is the profound revelation of the *incarnation*, a theological term describing his secular existence. Our calling is to be *human* like Jesus whom we are invited to follow, but that does not mean we are to mimic his ancient peculiarities.

The shifting of the cultural paradigm is scary and fraught with dangers—like shooting the rapids! We are tempted by the drag of social inertia and tradition to give a spin to the "facts" that allows us to frame issues according to the old patterns. We find easy justification for our deep anxieties. Our "natural" inclinations predispose us against expressions of same-sex sexual affection. (I write as a strictly heterosexual male.) Our fear of the unfamiliar and different—which in this case is dubbed "homophobia"—heightens our emotional response. We appeal to the "slippery slope" argument that such changes will lead to uncontrolled licentiousness and the breakdown of the family. And we justify all of this by an appeal to the literal transcultural authority of Scripture without a careful analysis of the ancient context of its moral principles and taboos.

The Ancient Pattern

Before we leave the subject of cultural change, we need to take a further look at the ancient social-moral context in which sexual morality was developed in order to understand the distinct character of modern developments. Basic presuppositions about the nature of human existence and relationships—which conditioned sexual attitudes and determined morality in ancient cultures—were quite different from ours. So even if we literally say the same words and perform the same actions in the modern social context, they have different meanings and implications.

For example, in ancient Mediterranean cultures the male of the species was considered to be the consummate human reality in the "natural order" of things. Females were considered less human than males because they lacked a penis, and, as they thought, did not contribute anything to the creation of a fetus. Women played the submissive sexual role. They were valued because they carried the male "seed" that reproduced the race, and because they provided pleasure to the male. By the same token, the humanity of eunuchs, those of questionable gender, and those males whose genitals had been injured were likewise demeaned. The watermark of masculinity was sexual virility, the ability to dominate (a harem) and to produce offspring, and males were the epitome of humanity. This relative evaluation of males and females determined the social patterns and gender roles that account for ancient sexual morality. Thus polygyny—one husband having many wives—was accepted as a natural moral pattern. The male's right to promiscuous sex and divorce of a wife who displeased him was simply assumed. By the same token, it was shameful (immoral) for a male to assume the passive gender role of a female, and the act of sodomy by victorious warriors was calculated as a demeaning rape.

Of course, I am not saying anything new. I am only trying to help us understand how cultural changes affect the meaning and morality of what we do and say. When Jesus challenged the prerogatives of men based on such ancient assumptions about what is "natural," it caused consternation among his disciples (Matt 19:10–11); and many more such cultural assumptions have been overturned in the intervening centuries! Consider what happened to sexual morals when it was discovered that women also contribute to the production of the fetus, when they were no longer considered inferior to men and the property of their husbands, or when they were recognized as equal to men and given the right to control their own sexuality. These changes in themselves change the basic meaning of the sexual relationship and the moral basis for sex acts like sodomy and oral sex. Both of the latter are considered matters of private volition among heterosexuals today. They change the moral concept of "effeminacy" as unnatural when applied to males. It is no longer weird and shameful for boys to be "sissy," or for girls to be "tomboys."

This does not mean that "ancient" is automatically wrong and "modern" is always right. According to Scripture, both ancient and modern alike stand under the judgment of God. But ancient civilizations were notoriously dissolute and violent. Given the basic cultural assumptions in a patriarchal, polygamous culture, the violent sexual practices of shaming ones enemies, and the religious fertility rites that included same-sex practices, one must assume that the taboos of the ancient Hebrews against sodomy understood as the proscriptions of Yahweh were pertinent to the times! What it does mean is that in order to make authentic modern applications of the ancient proscriptions we need to ask why certain behaviors were considered unnatural and immoral by the ancients. It is not a matter of asking whether Scripture is the word of God, but how God's word to an *ancient* culture should be interpreted and applied in *modern* culture. And this requires an astute evaluation of modern cultural presuppositions, biological realities, and social relationships as well as those of the ancients.

Clinical Concepts of Sexuality

In the culture of the nineteenth and the earlier twentieth century overt homosexual expressions of affection were deemed immoral and even criminal. Then, as early as the late nineteenth century, psychiatrists like Sigmund Freud (1856–1939) began to view homosexuality as a medical and not a moral disorder and developed psychiatric therapies for its treatment. Sexual variants from the strictly heterosexual pattern of the majority were classed as "medical defects or mental disorders"—like spina bifida, Down syndrome, or clinical depression—and thus not moral defects. Well into the latter part of the twentieth century psychiatrists like Charles Socarides—a founder of the National Association for Research and Therapy of Homosexuality (NARTH)—still considered it a psychological disorder and classified it as a "sexual orientation disturbance," for diagnostic purposes.[2]

But by the end of the twentieth century the majority of psychiatric and social work counselors had come to the conclusion that a same-sex affectional orientation in itself was neither a physical, mental, nor personality disorder that needed therapy. (Of course, individuals with a homosexual self-identity remain under social pressure, and may suffer from personal anxiety and social maladjustment.) Research on the human brain and the human genome from the last quarter of the twentieth century to the present seems to indicate that variations in sexual attraction are "biologically" based (a term used to include genetic, pre- and postnatal physical and social influences, and not necessarily implying genetic determination), and as such should not be treated either as a mental illness or moral perversion. Thus the

2. Socarides, "The Sexual Deviations and the Diagnostic Manual."

conclusion is drawn that sexual orientation is a non-moral phenomenon, and homosexual behaviors should be decriminalized.

The call for normalizing variant sexual orientations and decriminalizing sodomy implies more than that same-sex orientation is to be understood as an errant psychological bias of otherwise heterosexually oriented individuals. It is a psycho-social predisposition whose behavioral expression should be socialized as a normal sexual variation and regulated accordingly—an implication that secular society has readily accepted in theory, but has been slow to implement. Emboldened by this development the gay and lesbian community became more vocal in owning its orientation ("coming out of the closet") demanding their political rights as citizens, and their moral and religious rights as full members of the church. This publicizing of the movement is often criticized in the churches as its "politicization," but it may just as properly be seen as the correction of social injustice.

The Significance of "Orientation" for Moral Evaluation

Thus far the Christian community has not come to an agreement on the import of the clinical perspective or an independent understanding concerning its theological and ethical significance. Indeed the pronouncements of the church seem to defer to the politically correct right or left positions following traditional precedents in the cultural path of least resistance. Much as in the civil rights movement the church has proved to be a taillight rather than a headlight marking a cultural trail for civil society! For all the claims of its scholars and preachers it has failed to present a kingdom alternative to the power politics of the civil order.

What seems to be generally overlooked by defenders of traditional cultural norms is the significant paradigm shift that has taken place in our modern ethical reasoning. The modern approach begins with a clinical examination rather than moral diagnosis based on traditional religious and cultural conventions.

It researches the empirical causation of variation in sexual orientation, which implies that sexual attraction and bonding, in itself, is nonmoral. It judges the moral character of same-sex behavior in the light of the biological (as defined above) orientation of the persons involved. It evaluates the moral character of sexual behavior by standards of social *abuse*, whether hetero- or homosexual, but the ethical lines of demarcation are not gender-specific.

Further, it assumes the essential human equality and rights of every individual, whether male or female, black or white, old or young, heterosexual or homosexual. These presuppositions refocus the question of moral opprobrium from the act itself to the act in its social context. It focuses on personal and social consequences—whether the behavior involves social and personal manipulation and abuse—rather than the literal proscriptions of an ancient culture.

In contrast to this modern clinical approach, ancient culture—which is the context for biblical sexual taboos—considered sexuality as sexual *behavior* (the act itself). This melds the meaning of sexuality and sex. And the moral evaluation of the sex act was based upon an estimate of the essential humanity, gender, and social status of the individuals involved. The ancients seem not to have thought of orientation as a human self-identity distinct from emotional attraction (passion). Or if it was recognized in physical actuality of anatomical variations such as "born eunuchs," it was considered a deformity. Individuals on what we today call the GLBT continuum were considered queer, effeminate, weird, defective, and, or morally perverse—somehow less than fully human. Judging from contemporary accounts of social behavior in the upper classes of Greco-Roman culture, the homosexual practice of active bisexually oriented males, while open to moral censure, seems not to have diminished their humanity in the eyes of their peers.

Sexual attraction was considered an emotional expression that the fully prudent male kept under control. Sexual passions that led to unnatural (irrational) behavior were considered shameful and immoral by virtue of the weakness of character they displayed. Indeed, in the culture of late antiquity, Christians like Saint Augustine considered "passions" themselves morally and rationally unworthy. Thus taboos were put in place to regulate the sexual *act* of genital intimacy to control the orientation (passion).

This raises the question whether orientation in its modern clinical sense has any role in evaluating the moral character of sexual behavior. Is sexuality a matter of our self-identity as humans in God's image, or is it defined simply by erotic behaviors or misbehaviors? Is it to be identified morally with human "passions," which traditional theology identified as sinful? Or should it be given a clinical definition, which implies a human predisposition of a small minority without moral implications?

Conservative religious culture has identified sexual orientation with human passions and original sin. NARTH has continued the Freudian diagnosis as a medical condition for which it claims that there is effective therapy. Some in the conservative tradition who are sensitive to the negative attitudes toward gays attempt to make clear moral distinctions between orientation and practice. But if orientation is viewed simply as sexual attraction (passion), and the moral character of the passion is judged by the social-cultural attitudes toward same-sex behavior, then it is difficult to see how the orientation itself is not morally suspect.

Thus the import of a clinical understanding of the orientation for determining the moral character of sexual behavior has become the disputed question. Sexuality by its very nature involves us in relationships. One might even call it an urge to relationship. Should, therefore, the moral and religious nature of same-sex affectional behavior be judged by the physical act itself, or by the ethical relationship constituted in the act? There are many relationships in which overt sexual behavior—whether hetero- or homosexually oriented—is morally inappropriate. Clearly acts of pederasty, ritual prostitution, violent abuse (rape), and irresponsible and predatory promiscuity are immoral. But is this true of the sexual act itself?

For those who believe in the God of the Bible, as I do, the restatement of the moral issue in terms of social and personal relationships rather than physical anatomy and sex acts is not a negation of the biblical taboos. Rather it is an interpretation and social adaptation to modernity in the spirit of Christ. It simply defines more precisely the compassionate nonviolent specifications of loving ones neighbor (and enemy) as oneself in the modern world.

It is this shift in the cultural paradigms and modern empirical biological evidence that suggests the need for a reevaluation of the cultural classification of sexual deviancy. We have too much information about the biological roots and nature of sexual variation to limit our evaluation of its normality or abnormality to premodern notions of the "natural," based on ancient notions of causation and demographic necessity. One can no longer simply classify all deviations in sexual orientation as unnatural, shameful "moral deviancy" unless, of course, one still accepts the premodern concepts of human nature, gender distinction, social morality, physical causality, and class designations in the social definition of humankind.

This is not to say that modern scientific information resolves the ethical question without further ado. It is a generally accepted ethical dictum that the *empirical* does not in itself establish the moral *ought*. The "is" of genetic variation and its role in sexual orientation does not *ipso facto* establish the "ought" of sexual practice. But it raises the question of the inherent nature and purpose of sexual relationships, and whether and in what sense same-sex sexual relationships are "unnatural" and should be declared immoral.

As I write this, the legal battle over California's "Proposition 8" banning same-sex marriages is in the news headlines, and religious forces on both sides are gearing up for a political battle to sway an eventual Supreme Court decision. While such a political decision is important in civil society, it should not determine the church's position on the subject. Not so long ago the state laws of Virginia forbade Blacks and Whites from marrying or worshipping together in organized congregations, and unfortunately the churches acquiesced. If, as Hauerwas and Willimon argue in *Resident Aliens*, "the political task of Christians is to be the church rather than to transform the world"[3] is correct, a position with which I resonate, preserving the political tradition defining marriage as intended in the American Constitution is not its main concern. Discerning and applying Jesus' kingdom pattern to the modern paradigmatic culture shift that has so changed our society is.

3. Hauerwas and Willimon, *Resident Aliens*, 38. The long subtitle is of particular interest in this case: *A Provocative Christian Assessment of Culture and Ministry for People Who Know That Something Is Wrong.*

3

Fall or Finitude: The Augustinian Framing of the Debate

THE AUGUSTINIAN TRADITION, WHICH HAS DOMINATED Western theological analysis, has complicated the question of sexuality's source and moral genus with its interpretation of the fall of Adam as a historical occurrence rather than as a human condition. God's image and intention is associated with the complementary genital structure of the first man and woman, and all same-sex erotic urges are considered moral flaws caused by the sin of the first human parents. This sharp distinction between humanity as created and humanity as sinful or fallen from its former perfect righteousness identifies exclusive heterosexuality with God's creation intent, and same-sex sexuality by default becomes a moral deficit.

Evaluation of this traditional theological analysis requires us to go beyond the simple word studies of biblical prooftexts to establish precisely what the text meant in its original setting, and whether the post-Nicaean theologians got it right. We must first deconstruct the theological traditions that lie behind us and then reconstruct in order to let the Bible speak its authentic word of grace to our time. Indeed, this work of deconstructing-reconstructing in the spirit of Christ is precisely the work of the Holy Spirit in the church.

In the sphere of sexual ethics I would argue that the fifth-century Augustinian paradigm of a corrupted humanity floundering in sexual concupiscence is not a correct frame for interpreting and applying biblical understandings of human sexuality. It assumes that sexual intimacy, even at its best, is morally dubious. It lauds celibacy as the pinnacle of Christian virtue and finds unacceptable any variation on the theme of procreation as the moral justification for sex. While this theological tradition has been tinkered with in contemporary evangelical theology, its ghost still haunts the church's ethical evaluation of sexuality. In our twenty-first century far too many ethical decisions have been based on traditional cultural values that simply do not reflect the best information now available.[1]

Already in the early centuries of the church the Eastern (Greek) tradition—represented for example in Gregory of Nyssa—emphasized the significance of human finitude and traced the origin of sin to the choice of a finite free will. Sexual passion was considered natural to finite human nature *as created*, that is, not as sinful. It was not identified as the consequence of corrupted biological nature. Sin was identified as the abuse or misuse of sexual passion, and not inherent in the erotic longings themselves. Sexual sin lies not in the satisfaction of the erotic physical orientation—either its hetero- or homosexual embodiment—but in its selfish, narcissistic abuse.[2] This tradition, while not speaking directly to the issues involved in the modern debate

---

1. There is a large volume of material describing and analyzing the historical precedents of Roman Catholic moral theology dating from Augustine and the early church. There was a spate of literature following the Vatican II ecumenical council in the late 1960s. Tatha Wiley, a scholar at the University of Saint Thomas, has written an insightful and quite readable review of this data in her chapter "*Humanae vitae*, Sexual Ethics, and the Roman Catholic Church," in Kamitsuka, *The Embrace of Eros*, 99–114.

2. In his *The Human Factor*, 128ff., Philip Hefner gives a brief but very helpful review of this development and its implications.

about homosexual orientation, opens the possibility of a theological evaluation different from that which has dominated western theology.

The Augustinian paradigm raises the question of the nature and scope of *original sin* and its effect on human development. This is true especially in evaluating the moral character of deviant sexual orientation, understood as attraction. Are variations in sexual attraction the result of a primordial sin that altered the physio-psychological reality of the human race at its source? Or do they stem from the imperfections of finitude in creatures formed in the image of their Creator? In a later section we will treat the nature of sin and its consequences in more detail.

What about the Fall?

While Roman Catholic orthodoxy and conservative Protestantism differ on particulars in their interpretation of the Fall, both theologies follow Augustine in their framing presuppositions and semantic terminology underlying concepts of sexuality and arguments against homosexuality. The theological language and categories used to analyze the moral difference between orientation and practice of same-sex sexual relations follow the psychological and ethical categories used to describe the Fall and its effect.

It is not my intent to argue for or against the doctrine of original sin and moral depravity. Those who have lived through the twentieth century have witnessed the shifting battle between liberal and conservative theology, which need not be reviewed here. However, because orthodox Protestantism and Roman Catholicism are the main religious forces energizing the conservative Christian position in the culture wars of our present American society, it is important to examine further the semantic, hermeneutic, and rational assumptions and definitions that are presupposed.

Both Catholic and Protestant traditions describe the direct consequences of the Fall as physical suffering and death, psychological disorientation, and distortion of spiritual attitude and relationship to God, all of which are transmitted from generation to generation by sexual procreation. Rebellious bodily appetites that become the occasion for sin are aroused. These appetites are "temptations" to moral evil caused by sinful disorientation, and while they may not be sinful if resisted, they share the suspicion of moral perversion that has infected the psychophysical order of creation.

Adam and Eve were created perfect, "in the image of God," but their disobedience caused an ontological distortion in their essential humanity. One Lutheran theologian of the sixteenth century (Flacius Illyricus) even made the radical assertion that they exchanged the image of God for the image of the devil. Although not described in such stark terms, orthodoxy of the following centuries has maintained that the original "corruption" (John Calvin's term) is inheritable and it has "perverted the whole order of nature in heaven and on earth." Even the highest and most perfect physical and intellectual human types are "depraved" or morally corrupted.

Some early commentators even suggested that the knowledge forbidden to the first humans was sexual knowledge, hinting that the ruin of Eden, as of Camelot, was the fulfillment of erotic desire in sexual intercourse. Consequently the depravity of the human race is associated with sexuality and sexual perversion. By the early Middle Ages concupiscence or sexual lust became the primary moral manifestation of depravity rather than, for example, violence and greed.

According to this picture the putative sinful corruption is innate and includes the physical anomalies of birth—including culturally deviant sexual orientations—as well as moral and spiritual degeneracy. It accounts for the many physically, mentally, and morally imperfect specimens of humanity that have been born into the world. Indeed, it gives a moral cast to all human imperfections. The original human pair living before the Fall is the single example of moral and rational perfection, and represents the original intention or ideal against which sinful humanity is to be evaluated.

In this interpretative tradition the idea of God's original intention is virtually equated with the "natural," and perversion resulting from original sin with the "unnatural." And conversely the unnatural is identified as arrogant rejection of God's original intention. This cultural amalgam of the unnatural and moral perversity, which has exacerbated the ongoing controversy, is highly dubious. While there may be moral overlap in these designations, it should be noted that natural and unnatural are designations of cultural preference and tradition, and not classifications of sinful or immoral practice. There are wide variations in what human societies consider natural, which may or may not have moral implications across cultures.

Strange culturally deviant practices, tastes, and moral values, which may not in fact be sinful or ethically offensive, are often facilely identified as shameful, disgusting, and unnatural. Many of us who recall the early twentieth century remember when even an innocent trait like left-handedness was still considered unnatural, and the use of the left hand for writing was strongly discouraged. And until recent decades miscegenation was considered by many to be immoral and unbiblical. Given the still dominant Puritanical and Victorian sexual bias, it is not surprising that variant gender self-identities and sexual preferences are considered shameful perversions of the *natural order*. And it is easy for those who interpret and apply Scripture literally to find cultural precedents in selected texts of the Bible that support this bias.

So how are we to define "original sin," and understand its effect on the human image of God? Does it include the corruption of nature that affects the biological realm of genetics? Is it a corruption passed from generation to generation by sexual indulgence? Does it account for deviations from heterosexuality in sexual orientation so that by their very existence they are morally suspect? How we answer these questions depends partly upon our definition of sin and immorality.

Except for those commentators who are still persuaded by scientific, theological, and moral biases of earlier centuries, the first chapters of Genesis are not understood to be scientific historical accounts. Rather, they are understood as narratives of *prehistorical beginnings* that describe in story form God's intention for human life and history, and the failure of every generation beginning with the first to fulfill that intention. The Fall, or original sin, describes the human condition in which the loss of innocence through self-assertion cannot be traced to a chronologically identified premeditated act. It is "original" in the sense that it is not a consciously acquired characteristic through deliberate choice. The inherent character of the misstep becomes evident in the predictable but unanticipated alienation that inevitability occurs.

Sin is not a state of psychosomatic corruption. It is not, as I wrote in *God Our Savior*, "equated with creaturely limitation or with the reflexes and desires of the physical body. It is not the kind of desire one can overcome by ascetic disciplines, such as yogic breath control, fasting, and muscular contortions." And in this present context I might add by therapeutic counseling, spiritual formation, and sexual self-discipline. "Sin is an existential and relational concept, not an essential and ontic one."[3] Sin is a haughty prideful attitude, a posture toward God and others that disrupts, abuses, and alienates us from them. Sin is a perversion of relationship that disrespects the worth of the other made in God's image. It should not be identified with specific acts, which in different cultures and situations can and do have different personal meanings.

An Evangelical Option

The Western theological tradition, stemming from Augustine, has tended to identify all sexual desire as sinful cupidity or

3. Kraus, *God Our Savior*, 125.

lust, which is a consequence of the sin of the first human pair. According to Augustine, only the possibility and intention of procreation mitigates the sin of sexual arousal and its gratification. The desire itself, both heterosexual and homosexual, is morally tainted. Based strictly on Augustine's argument, *heterosexual sex using contraception is just as sinful as homosexual sex*, and same-sex erotic desire in and of itself is illicit with no moral excuse since it is desire for that which has no justifiable end. The desire itself is sinful, and it must be dealt with as moral weakness and temptation. Evangelical Protestants still implicitly appeal to this Augustinian evaluation of erotic sexual desire although they do not follow his logic when they justify the use of contraceptives in heterosexual intercourse.

In this tradition, the sexual union of man and woman, while sinful because of the desire (lust) that leads to it and accompanies it, may be morally excused if the intent is procreation. Indulgence of the desire cannot be morally justified under *any other* condition. Following this logic conservative Protestant evangelicals insist that marriage be defined only as a heterosexual pairing for the ostensible purpose of bearing children. But, in contrast to Augustine, their quite modern insistence on the romantic spiritual character of erotic heterosexual intimacy and approval of contraception throw into question traditional arguments that have defined the morality of sex. Whether intended or not, these exceptions create an implicit possibility for the moral and spiritual reevaluation of all sexual intimacy and the redefinition of family relationships.

Conservative Protestant ethicists continue to reference Augustine's concept of the Fall as the biblical perspective for defining sexual morality but do not identify erotic sexual desire itself as sin. They continue to frame the issues of sexual orientation in terms of moral perversion: *perverted* desire for heterosexual partners is sin, and same-sex attraction *is* sinful perversion. Whether honorable sexual desire for a same-sex partner is morally perverted and to be repented of has become the focus of debate. Is desire for erotic same-sex relationship sin, or to be considered a temptation, which if resisted is not sin? This ambiguous classification of the attraction and its sharp distinction from erotic fulfillment continues to frame the issue.

The moral distinction between "attraction" as temptation that is not in itself sinful if resisted and "practice," which is ambiguously defined as sexual activity beyond the comfort level of the heterosexual majority, remains ethically and theologically ambiguous. For practical ecclesial purposes, *practice* is roughly defined as genital intercourse and the moral fulcrum is placed at the point of volitionally controlled action. Nevertheless, the taint of illicit desire or attraction remains morally problematic and is often compared to personal weaknesses like alcoholism, pedophilia, and the *temptation* to sadomasochism, pornography, and other physical and character malfunctions that may be attributed to the sin of Adam.

Obviously personal human nature and social relationships are imperfect and flawed by *actual* sin. But was Adam's misstep a "fall" from perfection? Does the Augustinian paradigm of creation's debasement and humankind's moral depravity caused by Adam's sin provide the proper template for understanding human sexuality in all its variety? Rather, does not the original story presuppose humankind's vulnerability to mistakes, decay, and death? Eden, as described in Genesis, is not the state of perfection but of finite innocence, which implies imperfection. As Hefner summarizes it, "it is not the 'bad' or uncontrollable dimension of human sexuality and culture that conveys sin, but rather the human constitution as such, including those elements that make for human distinctiveness and goodness."[4]

In fact, the whole biblical narrative assumes that creation is the beginning of an eschatological plan terminating in perfection, not beginning with it. Paul in 1 Corinthians 15 refers to Adam as "from the earth made of dust" in contrast to Jesus as the heavenly pattern of God's image. If we assume a finite creation, which

4. Hefner, *The Human Factor*, 140.

the Genesis account clearly does, then we must assume that the original human parents were neither perfect nor immune from multiple divergent possibilities, that is, modifications for better or worse. Their mammalian bodies surely were subject to procreant deviation, and the sexual self-identities of their progeny open to sexual variations of the kind we observe in humankind.

The phenomenon of intersexuality and gender ambiguity, which until very recently has been little understood, seems clearly to indicate that sexual diversity stems from the limitation and irregularities of finite possibilities rather than moral corruption. The technical possibility of analyzing the chromosomal make-up of the body's cells reveals that there are a variety of karyotype combinations other than the standard XX and XY that define female and male. The ancient pictures of Hermaphrodites, the mythical double-sexed freak or goddess, is slowly giving way to a more informed picture of a human biological and psychological condition that occurs approximately once in every 2,000 births.

Thus we should not assume that all physical and psychological human imperfections, blemishes, and deficiencies are the result of an antediluvian self-inflicted moral corruption (fall from perfection) rather than inherent finitude. The ancients were quite aware that to be finite is to be imperfect in knowledge and power, and thus subject to variation! The fatal error of the fundamentalistic Augustinian tradition of recent centuries is that it assumes finite creatures—Adam and Eve—were created perfect, not just innocent. Here Paul Tillich's coalescing of the creation and fall symbolism is a valid insight into the nature of the biblical view of the universe and humankind.[5] From the beginning, imperfect human beings have moved in uneven stages from innocence through developing moral and spiritual discrimination.

5. Tillich writes, "The transition from essence to existence is not an event in time and space but the transhistorical quality of all events in time and space. This is equally true of man and of nature. 'Adam before the Fall' and 'nature before the curse' are states of potentiality. They are not actual states." *Systematic Theology,* vol. 2, 40.

The uneven trajectory is clear in the story of ancient Israel under the tutelage of Yahweh.

Framing the issue of same-sex *orientation* within the context of finite imperfection rather than moral corruption is crucial to determining the moral character of same-sex erotic *behavior*. If we define the image of God in terms of physical anatomy, what one Dutch scholar called a "genital view of sexuality,"[6] or hold as Robert Gagnon puts it, that an essential part of the image is the biological "complementary male and female anatomy,"[7] any deviation from this normative physical image is always a perversion of nature, and its erotic consummation a sinful human rebellion against God.

If we frame the question of variant sexualities, not in terms of a moral perversion, but as a matter of finitude and imperfection, the concept of orientation, which is at the crux of the debate, becomes by definition an amoral self-identity and not perverted desire for the anatomically similar. As with all human sexuality, exclusive heterosexual identity included, it is not the genital configuration of the partner that determines the moral legitimacy of the attraction or its fulfillment in mutual respect and affection.

This is not to argue that innate disposition or genetic influence excuse immoral choices. The question is what defines choices as immoral, and from a Hebrew Christian perspective the moral distinctive does not reside in the sexual or gender identity of the human partner. Rather it is the will of God for *shalom* in the human family that reflects the image of the Trinity. We will look at this in more detail later. All the moral qualifications that define genuine loving personal relationship apply across all aspects of sexual behavior. And in turn all the immoral characteristics of any sexual act—such as abuse, promiscuity, unfaithfulness, lack of mutuality, and the like—apply equally.

While in general we make moral distinctions between instinctive feelings, attractions, or desires and choice to act upon

6. J. van Ussel quoted in Pronk, *Against Nature*, 157.

7. Gagnon, *The Bible and Homosexual Practice*. 58.

them, in this case the desire and act cannot so easily be separated for moral evaluation. Our sexuality is of such a nature that it is realized, as Bruce Hiebert has noted in a MennoNeighbors [*sic*] e-mail, in the "embodiment of desire and act," whether that act is a fleeting thought, a furtive glance, affectionate gesture, or genital consummation.[8] Orientation in this case denotes a finite mode of being that is defined in doing, which may be thinking, desiring, resisting desire or fulfilling it in physical-social behavior. And all such chosen behavior is subject to the same moral requirements. Our instinctual reflexes and predispositions define who we are as sexual beings. And every sexual orientation, including the "straight," is imperfect and tempted to moral perversion.

---

8. Jakobsen and Pellegrini perceptively point out that religion and sexuality have this in common. "But religion is no more reducible to what an individual believes than sexuality is contained by what an individual 'is.' There must be space for practice, for enactment, in both individual and communal contexts. Where both religion and sex are concerned, performance is constitutive of identity" (Jakobsen and Pellegrini, *Love the Sin*, 126). This is a valid insight whether or not one accepts their total argument for relaxing the moral and legal restrictions on sexual behavior.

4

Sex and the Image of God: Biblical Framework

THE EXALTED CONCEPT THAT HUMAN BEINGS ARE FORMED in the image and likeness of God has its origin in the creation myths of Genesis—quite in contrast, we may add, to the creation myths of some of Israel's neighbors. While the image concept is never analyzed in either the Old or the New Testaments, it is everywhere presupposed. It is carried forward by the concept of Yahweh as Father and Israel as his children, and the children are to be in the parent's likeness. It is important to note that the image is a mark of human self-identification and not a description of God. When we say that human sexual self-consciousness is intrinsic to that image, we do not mean to imply that God shares in physical sexuality. In both its life and worship Israel guarded carefully against the idea that Yahweh is a sexual deity like the gods of the nations around them. This is the reason that we must carefully decipher the image and likeness of God in which we humans share.[1]

1. The image metaphor is reflexive. It begins with a "given" (revealed) self-conceptualization of humans in society, which in turn is projected onto God. Not until Jesus, the Messiah, is such a projection thought to be embodied on the human scene (John 1:14). Then in a counter-reflexive turn this highest human concept of deity is applied to human self-conceptualization. The metaphor is not of individual male machismo, but of a Jesus–like character projected onto God. When in later Christian theology the trinitarian concept of God's true nature is developed it becomes the divine reality from which the

40

Differing concepts of the image, creation, and original sin depend upon one's reading of the original creation narratives. As we have noted in the framework of Augustinian theology and the interpretations of some ancient rabbis, these accounts have been understood as literal historical accounts, namely, a historical succession of the creation of perfect human creatures followed by sinful disobedience of God's prohibition to eat of the tree of knowledge that caused the consequent depravity of the human race. This interpretation begins with the assumption that the perfect image of God included the divinely created biological structures of heterosexual "human anatomy and procreative functions."[2] There is good reason to doubt that this etiological interpretation of the stories as historical is a correct frame for the universal theological and moral condition of humans today.

Each of the Genesis stories of human origins presents a different slant, but they all clearly reflect the strong cultural bias of the ancient Hebrew culture. For example, at the birth of her firstborn, Cain, Eve's self-justification of womanhood reflects this bias. "I have produced a man [male] with the help of the Lord," she exults (Gen 4:1). And the text adds, "Next she bore his brother Abel." But is this bias to be equated with the eternal and universal will of Yahweh? Is a woman's feminine humanity to be judged by childbearing, and a man's masculinity to be judged by his sexual potency? Are women valued chiefly for their ability to bear children? Are eunuchs and those with damaged genitalia, who were despised and excluded from temple worship, to be avoided by the church? And shall other sexual variants be accepted only with special restrictions? Should we not rather consider male machismo with its presumptions claims to superiority and self-serving definitions of gender and sexual roles, which give rise to abusive treatment of women and sexually deviant fellow humans, a consequence of depravity?

---

metaphorical description of humanity evolves.

2. This exact wording comes from Gagnon, *The Bible and Homosexual Practice*, 259, but its virtual parallel can be found in many scholarly treatises.

These stories, which both the Jewish and Christian religions consider revelation of God's true intent for human life and history, are communicated through the filter of ancient Hebrew historical experience. They seek to explain how and why family relationships experienced in Hebrew society are what they are.[3] But while the sexual values of the ancient Hebrews seem to be assumed, the taboos of the holiness code are not for the most part explicitly linked to the stories of human origin. Disobedience to God's covenant is linked to increased difficulty in birthing for the female, and drudgery of labor for the male, plus physical death for both, none of which are exclusively Hebrew. Only the patriarchal dominance to which Eve must submit suggests an etiological explanation of the gender relationships of men and women in Hebrew society. This, however, is not so much etiological as mimetic. As Hosea observes, the changed relation in family patterns was effected by a changed relation to God: from "husband" to "dictator" (Hos 2:16–18). The continuing faithlessness of Israel following Adam's example has resulted in their dehumanization—violence, adultery, idolatry, greed, and the like (Hos 6:7).

In fact, the Genesis stories say little or nothing about a cultural morality of sex, although the effects of sin are reflected in the violence, polygamy, idolatry, and abuse in the following chapters. In contrast to the myth of Aristophanes in Plato's *Symposium*,[4] for example, the subject of sexual variation and its regulation is not within the purview of the stories. They describe

3. Ken Stone and other scholars identify these stories as "etiological discourse," which means that they begin with the assumption that human reality is as experienced in the ancient setting. See Thistlethwaithe, *Adam, Eve,* 117-26.

4. In his myth to explain sexual variation Aristophanes said that the first human figures were joined back to back, some male to male, others male to female, and female to female before Zeus split them apart. Thus sexual attractions are the longing to find one's original gender bond. Except for Paul's reference to pagan examples (Rom 1:26) the Bible makes no mention of feminine same-sex liaisons and such etiology, and treats sodomy as rape to humiliate the enemy, and pagan sacramental symbol to activate the gods. Both are thoroughly condemned!

human mammals made in God's image as innately sexual, and imply that sexual reproduction along with management of the created order is part of the evidence for the image (Gen 1:26–28; 2:20b–24). They speak of the nature of humanity and its relation to a divine Creator, but they do not elaborate a cultural religious pattern.[5] Even the benchmark of monogamous marriage—with which I fully agree—is at most *implied* in the story of Eve's creation as Adam's suitable partner. And while they recognize the innate centrality of sexuality to human identity, they do not enunciate a specific code of sexual morality that can be used to regulate variant sexual orientations. Rather, they suggest that we must recognize our innate tendency to act in our own self-interest even under the most favorable circumstances—perhaps especially when we are most certain of our moral superiority.

This being so, just as it is incorrect to interpret the individual characters and events of the stories as the literal beginning of the human race, it is improper to insist on a universal literal transplanting of the cultural-moral patterns that the stories reflect. To put this in theological terms, sin must not be equated with the literal ritual and moral taboos of the Old Testament narrative.

If we speak of the human condition, in Calvin's terms, as "depravity" resulting from original sin, it is, as he said, a *total* depravity in the sense that *all facets of human life and relations are affected by it*. It describes the totality of human relations and values. The highest human moral values of justice, righteousness, and holiness are affected. Indeed, the study of world cultures from ancient times to the present leaves the impression of partiality and self-serving even in the highest moral codes. And this

---

5. In the biblical narrative we must wait for the priestly codes of Leviticus—which most biblical scholars locate late in Israel's historical interaction with other cultures during the dispersion—to find explicit regulations for sexual behavior. In that setting the regulations clearly represent a Hebrew-Jewish protest against the idolatry and abuse that seems to have characterized the nations around them. Our point here is that these passages, which are constantly used as the theological grounding for heterosexual monogamy, actually do not explicitly address that issue.

is perhaps most obvious in the area of human sexuality and family relationships. Rather than moral commitment, love, and integrity as the norm for evaluating personal sexual relationships, such cultural values as machismo and sexual potency, the abundance of progeny, cultural gender definitions, sexual identity of the partners, and the like have been used. And in all too many instances biblical texts reflecting the ancient cultural norms of Israel are quoted to substantiate such use, as though God's final word is identified with Hebrew taboos.

I have called attention to this variety and lack of explicit reference to etiological sexual regulations in the original text, not to argue that the texts approve variant sexual practices, but merely to call attention to the degree to which our contemporary reading of the text is vulnerable to implicit current attitudes and assumptions. It leaves the modern interpreter vulnerable to reading current cultural biases and theological interpretations into the text. Not only is the textual material culture specific in its bias, but it leaves many of the sexual questions being raised in our modern culture to be answered implicitly. This raises the question of cross-cultural contextual adaptation: whether the implications of the text must be read and applied only according to its original culture specific bias. At least one renowned Jewish commentator has suggested that precisely because the Levitical regulations are so culture specific they do not apply directly to Gentiles.[6]

If we interpret the consequences of the first couple's disobedience as the marring of the image of God, then we must understand it as a rupture in relationship with the Creator-Sustainer of the universe that seriously affects human community. Understood this way these stories suggest that the issue at stake is *shalom* in interpersonal relations, that is, an attitude or orientation and social structure that discourages selfish disregard of the true worth of others and maximizes compassionate responsibility for the whole human community.

6. See Milgrom, *Leviticus*, 1567–68.

Interpreting the Image of God

The possibility of diversity in sexual orientation is not explicitly spoken to in these Genesis accounts. In the first story of creation (Gen 1:1—2:3) the image is explicitly identified with humanity in personal sexual relationship ("male and female") and with the command to establish human dominance and regency over the earth. In the second story (Gen. 2:15–25) the image is not complete until a suitably human partner is created. None of the mammalian creatures created independently are suitable as sexual soulmates. Adam must have a fully human counterpart who answers to his own self-identity, and the basic concern is the propagation of humanity in God's image. Thus special surgery by God to excise woman from the human creature already in existence was necessary. Adam could truly say she is flesh of my flesh and bone of my bone. As in the first story, *human* sexual fulfillment is possible only in a fully human relationship. The conclusion in verses 24–25 that a man shall leave his father and mother and cling to his wife suggests further that the propagation of the human image of God is a priority concern.

Both accounts, as we might expect, clearly reflect the ancients' concern for posterity and dominance over the animal population as they assume the parameters for community propagation. The default mode for human sexuality is male-female complementarity for the propagation of the race, but the question of human sexual variation is not broached. If a broader taboo is intimated, it would be prohibition of sexual relations with animals other than humans (Lev 20:15–16). It is doubtful whether this default mode should be read to define and regulate all the possibilities for permissible individual sexual relationships between humans until the end of time.

Nevertheless, the clear inference is that humanity shares a sexual consciousness inherent in their human self-identity. Thus the question of sexual orientation must be considered part of the theological, or in philosophical language, ontological definition of humans in the image of God. We are not simply dealing with moral-legal classifications of social-political deviations. Especially in the church, therefore, empirical realities of sexual variations should be dealt with at a more discriminating level than mere psychological evaluation, moral prohibition, and social control.

Perhaps the most common misperception of the "image of God, *male and female*" in Genesis 1:26–27 is reflected in the way we usually speak of it as an image *in individual* humans. But the account clearly says that humans, or better, *humanity* was made "in God's image," not that God's image was deposited in individual humans. Humankind in its physical-social embodiment was formed *in* the image of God. The picture is not of the image of God implanted as a distinct spiritual essence into fleshly humankind. The image is not a divine spark or immortal spiritual energy embedded in an individual mammalian creature named Adam. It did not turn Adam into a dualistic creature part divine rational spirit and part earthly physical sexual body. It is not a divine spark of rationality or immortal spirit as in the Greek philosophical tradition. Rather, the image points to a sexual reality beyond that of individual genetic karyotypes to a relational image.

In tribal cultures, such as the Bible assumes, individual self-identity is ineluctably attached to communal identity and is received through one's relation to and participation in the familial group. An individualistic or idiosyncratic identity is a rogue identity, and in such a cultural context the image metaphor undoubtedly refers to individuals-in-human-community. Thus individuals share in the image as they are recognized sons and daughters of the familial or tribal *people of God*.

This family process of recognizing and naming is alluded to in Genesis 5 where the story of humankind's creation in God's image is repeated. Adam's life is recounted as the time before *"he became father of a son in his likeness, according to his image*, and named him Seth" (v. 3). And the remaining days of his life are counted "after he became the father of Seth," Seth being the one in the genealogy who continues the line of the image, not Cain or the deceased Able. The individual image of God recognized in Seth is a spiritual or personal capacity to respond to the family's recognition and identification of the family likeness. We call this reciprocal relation of "father/mother and son/daughter," which identifies and nurtures the image, love (*eros, agape, philia*). And it is this loving, nonviolent relationship that in turn determines the moral nature of all family relationships including the sexual.

This family image indicates what we today refer to as *person* or personal being, which is grounded in sexual, self-conscious identity fully realized only in reciprocated relationships with others in human community. This clearly implies that the question of sexual orientation needs to be related to the realization of the image of God *in human community*, and not simply to individual Homo sapiens. Theologically considered, sexual orientation is not merely an erotic physical passion, but a self-defining longing for relationship with others equally human. And this in biblical language is called "the image of God," which is after the pattern of God's own triune *being in community*.

The personal image is at once social and individual. The image defines humans as *covenant animals*. In comparison to Aristotle's concept of humans as individual "rational animals" who can form political organizations for their advantage, the concept of covenant community suggests that full human potential is realized only in mutually covenanted relationships of respect and integrity under the parenthood of God. It is fully realized in the covenanted human community under the benevolent sovereignty of God's bounty, and individuals share that image as they participate in community. Of course, personal self-consciousness, rationality, free will, ability to recognize and obey law, and the like are clearly implied in the covenant commands that are given by God. But the emphasis is upon the relation to God the Creator and Sustainer as a collective "people," not on individual human abilities. In like manner emphasis is upon the ability of human community to continue God's creative acts in the procreation of the image, and not on the morality of private sex.

This concept of God's image reflected in the human family is strengthened by the Christian concept of God as personal Trinity. Many ontological characteristics of God such as rationality, immortality, and creative power have been suggested as that in God which corresponds to the metaphorical analogy of the image. But taking our clues from the New Testament, and without making a detailed philosophical analysis, we learn that God is a personal unity of trinitarian relations. *In a word, God is the ontological embodiment of loving relationship, which on earth is to be embodied in the nonviolent human community of shalom— love, justice, and peace.*

In a chapter entitled "The Practical Trinity," Catherine Mowry LaCugna wrote that because the doctrine of the Trinity "uses the idea of 'person' and 'relation' to affirm that God is essentially personal and relational, the doctrine of the Trinity is also the foundation for a theology of the human person, and a theology of right relationship." And she continues, "because it affirms that persons, whether divine or human, are made to exist in loving communion with one another, *the doctrine of the Trinity is also the foundation for the vision of society and a vision of the church which is to be a sign to the world of the ultimate destiny of all creatures*" (italics mine). The image, as she states so well, is contained in the "mystery of persons in relationship."[7]

A second common assumption that is made when the image is associated with individual identity is that it implies complementary sexual gender, that is, as we have noted in Robert Gagnon's writings, anatomical or biological complementarity. Interpreted this way the image becomes an argument for exclusive heterosexuality as the sole reflection of the image of God. Any other explicitly sexual relations are considered a perversion of God's original intention. And since same-sex attraction is by

7. Collins, *Exploring Christian Spirituality*, 279.

their definition unnatural, the protestations of those with such orientation to feelings of affection, love, and admiration are discounted as evidence for genuine self-identity.

But more recent research that takes seriously the experience of transsexuals and other sexual identities throws serious question on this biological model of the image of God. Pastor and family counselor Eric Swenson's account in the *Christian Century*, for example, of his efforts to realize and live openly as the person he knew himself to be, even after years of marriage and begetting children, needs to be entered as theological data.[8] What is overlooked in the equation of image and sex complementarity are the rich interpersonal dimensions of complementary human sexuality and the psychosomatic quality of erotic sexual intimacy implied in the image. Gender identities and physical identities do not always match. This, of course, is not a new observation, but past social cultural patterns of sexual and gender identities have often been demeaning and harmful, and the church's treatment of persons of transgender and transsexual identity has often been insensitive and inhospitable.

Image in the New Testament

The references to the image of God in the New Testament are mainly christological and not anthropological. Jesus, not Adam, reflects the true image. The one explicit exception is found in 1 Corinthians 11:7–9, where Paul says that males are the "image and reflection of God; but woman is the reflection of man [male]." Apparently his reference is to the second creation account in Genesis 2, and he seems to be unaware of the Matthean tradition that understood Jesus to say they share equally the image. We will look in more detail at the Matthew 19 passage.

In his discussion of the resurrection in 1 Corinthians 15, Paul speaks of Jesus as the authentic ("heavenly/spiritual")

8. Swenson, "Becoming Myself," 28–33.

human pattern in whom and through whom the authentic image of God is realized. By contrast Adam is a finite "living being" from the earth and made of dust. He is the finite psychosomatic pattern subject to death in whose image we all are formed by birth. The other references are principally to Jesus as the Christ who is the visible image and glory of God (2 Cor 4:4; Col 1:15). These allude to a theological picture of Jesus who in the form of God humbled himself to become human (Phil 2:5–8).

When the creation stories describe the present human situation, they symbolizes authentic human reality in its finite innocence, and as the biblical story continues it becomes clear that even this unmarred relationship with God is an eschatological reality—the end toward which God's creative purpose is moving. It describes the human family in "the image of the man of dust" (1 Cor 15:49) before its renewal in "the image of its creator." The story of the Fall represents what Tillich called the existential actualization of the image on the way to transformation, which is imaged in the Christ as "the new being."[9]

Where the image metaphor is used of humankind it is spoken of as a "new self . . . renewed in knowledge according to the image of its creator" (Col 3:10–11). According to this passage the renewal results in an ethical and social unity in Christ where traditional religious and moral taboos and national and social identities no longer hinder the accomplishment of God's *shalom*. Jesus is the authentic ("heavenly") human in whom and through whom the image is realized (1 Cor 15:48).

With this in mind note how Jesus emphasized the personal/spiritual dimensions of behavior in contrast to ritual and legal regulations, cultic ceremony, and cultural and social biases. As examples, he recognized and responded to the faith of Gentiles. He touched and healed the untouchables who approached him. He acknowledged and blessed the despised *eunouchoi*. He

---

9. While Tillich did not frame his analysis in eschatological terms, his existentialist terminology is helpful in imaging the relation between creation and fall. See Tillich, *Systematic Theology*, vol. 2.

pronounced Sabbath observance relative to human welfare. He honored the full human worth of women, even those excluded by their peers. He made progeny second to faithful covenant relation in the case of marital divorce. Cultural tradition, social bias, and moral judgment according to the Law, all took second place to integrity and compassion.

Jesus—God's "Original Intention"

Many commentators and preachers have used Jesus' saying in Matthew 19:3-6 concerning God's original intention for husband and wife to argue against same-sex marital partnerships. Such an argument is based on the implicit assumption that the image of God is expressed in the anatomical complementarity of male and female. With an attempt at wry humor some preachers have noted that the Genesis account says "Adam and Eve" and not "Adam and Steve." On the surface this exegesis may seem persuasive, but a closer look at the textual and cultural context and the nuance of the Pharisees' challenge throws doubt on the dogmatic certainty of the interpretation.

In contrast to the parallel saying in Matthew 5:31-32 the conversation with the Pharisees in chapter 19 hangs on the phrase *"for any reason,"* and the reaction of the shocked disciples as well as the following reference to the status of eunuchs (vv. 10-12) indicates that more than the legality of divorce is at issue in this context. The more consequential issue has to do with the social and religious status of different sexual identities, namely, women, eunuchs, and children, that were considered inferior and without acceptance as full participants in the human community.

To catch the nuance of Jesus' answer to the Pharisees' question about divorce it is important to note that he primarily appealed to the first Genesis account of the creation story and not the second. In the beginning, Jesus says, humans were created "male *and female* [in God's image]"; and these two are "one flesh" (not as in the second Genesis account where woman is created from the man's rib as a servant-companion more adequate than any other mammalian creature). The Pharisaic interpretation of woman's place in the social order seems clearly to assume the second story.

Further, the *man* is to leave his original family to be joined to his wife in an equal union of "one flesh." The text clearly implies that the original design was not for women to leave their heritage family and join the husband's family as second-class citizens, the pattern of much of the ancient world! The emphasis here is on the status of women as full and equal participants in the human family and not on the biological sexual union of husband and wife as we are so want to interpret it in our modern sex-saturated culture.

It is obvious that the passage assumes what is called in computer language "the default position" of heterosexual marriage. That is implicit in the question itself, which also limits the scope of its applicability to the issues at hand. Neither the question nor the answer addresses the question of sexual orientation. We might also note that the answer does not explicitly address the question of monogamous marriage, that is, whether the husband has a right to take a second wife without divorcing the first.

The question assumes the inferior status and rights of women, and the husband's assumed right to certified progeny by the woman of his choosing. Jesus' answer should be read in that cultural context. His reply that God created humankind "male and female" rejects the insinuation of woman's innate inferiority implied in the divorce legislation. And his rejection of divorce at the whim of the husband rejects the husband's assumed right to divorce a woman who does not bear him children. According to verse 9 only sexual unfaithfulness of a wife, which raised questions about the certainty of a husband's paternity, might justify divorce.

The force of Jesus' answer then, first of all, establishes woman's equality and the priority of the wife's status and welfare ahead of the husband's right to progeny. In a social order where men had an unquestioned right to progeny, even if it meant adding a second wife to the family circle or divorcing his wife in order to marry another, Jesus says clearly that apart from sexual unfaithfulness of the wife there are no grounds for a husband to desert his wife and marry another. Again reflecting the cultural context, the disciples' stunned reaction establishes this reading of the text.

In response to the disciples' incredulity Jesus suggested that perhaps not all males could accept the new implications of male-female equality, but he presses the issue even further. Equality as fellow humans in the image of God also includes eunuchs. They are to be respected and accepted into the covenant community and thus find their identity as part of God's family. This seems to be an allusion to the Isaiah 56:3–5 passage where God promises to give eunuchs who hold fast his covenant "a monument and a name better than sons and daughters" among God's people.

This reference to eunuchs, especially those "who have been so from birth" (v. 12), is more pertinent to evaluating the moral significance of variation in sexual orientation than the creation reference to male and female in God's image. Not all of his male hearers, Jesus says, can accept this teaching which requires a total reevaluation of the sexual role of the family, but he adds, "Let anyone accept this that can." The implication seems to be that the traditional family and sexual ideals and priorities are displaced by the new contingencies in the kingdom rule he has come to establish. The new canon for judging sexual and family morality, as in the letters of Paul, is the priority of the kingdom of God.

While this gives us no explicit guidance for dealing with sexual variation in the church, it strongly suggests that in the kingdom of God the primary goal of marriage is not biological progeny. Jesus' acceptance of individuals despised in the old order for their sexual variance and impotence clearly shifts the premises for evaluating human sexual relations. It challenges conventional "family values," which his contemporary Jewish audience and many of the current Christian Right still assume.

Adam Who? Theological Framing of Texts

The human referent of the image metaphor has significant implications for understanding the theological meaning of individual human sexual variation. If Adam—male and female created in God's image—refers to the man and woman as a sexual pair, one might argue that the account infers that heterosexually oriented individuals are in the image, and same-sex oriented are not—or at least are a marred or perverted image. However, if that is done, many other questions are raised. For example, do celibate males and females, whether by choice or circumstance, only partially bear that image? And where do the developmentally impaired belong in the picture? What about "eunuchs" and others of uncertain gender identity who in the ancient world were called "effeminate" and considered defective humans?

However, as we have seen, the primary referent of the image metaphor is the social-spiritual human community, which in the New Testament is referred to as the new humanity, and not the individual mammalian creatures named Adam and Eve. Those who insist that the literal first male-female pair present, the only legitimate moral possibility for sexual coupling seem to have overlooked the possible implications of this crucial distinction. While the image in the creation stories includes physical sexual relationships, as we have noted, it is not defined by gender complementarity. Rather, it is the image which conditions the moral-personal character of physical sexual relations of whatever orientation. *The essential moral-personal character and significance of the erotic physical relation (sex) is conditioned by its personal spiritual character and not by its gender complementarity.* This implies further that the morality of physical erotic intimacies is not properly evaluated by the orientation of the partners, but by the moral quality of such physical relationships. In so far as physical sexual intimacy reflects and furthers human *shalom*, it participates in the image of God. In so far as it is abusive and destructive of human *shalom*, it is a desecration of the image of God. This is equally true of all sexual activity.

5

Theological Reflections: Divine *Eros* as the Image

THE SOCIAL ASPECT OF THE IMAGE METAPHOR HAS LONG
been recognized, as Thomas Finger, referencing the classic work
of H. Wheeler Robinson, points out in his *Self, Earth and Society*.
"Personal identity is so intertwined with group structure in
Hebrew Scripture that the former cannot exist without the latter."[1]
But the significance of its sexual connotations was not commonly
recognized in theology until the perspectives of feminist theology
insisted on the full humanity of women and men. This prompted
a more appreciative exploration of divine *eros* as the pattern for
understanding the social image.

Traditionally Christian theologies, following Stoic philosophical precedents, identified the image of God with the human
ability to reason and make moral choices. Also following Greek
precedent, they attributed this ability primarily to the individual
male, Adam. While biblical exegesis generally adds the theological dimension of communicating with God, and the mandate to
have dominion over the earth as part of the image, the assumption that the image applies primarily to the individual male continued. But an anthropological reading of the text of Genesis 1
in its reference to "male and female" indicates quite clearly that

1. Finger, *Self, Earth and Society*, 266.

Adam in the image of God is a *social* image. And the second account in chapter 2:23–24—"Therefore a man leaves his father
and his mother and clings to his wife, and they become one
flesh"—includes the formation of a familial community. While
the rational and volitional attributes of the individual creatures
are undoubtedly implicit in the metaphor, it describes a family
relationship that mirrors the relationship of Yahweh as Father-
Creator begetting in his own image.

From the first chapters of the Bible there is a vast contrast
between the cultural images of God in Hebrew literature and that
of their neighbors—for example, the mythical descriptions of
Baal, Zeus, and Yahweh—and this difference is what the Hebrews
understood as God's *holy image*, which is spelled out in narrative depiction and ritual regulations. To be human is to be God's
child and share in inherited family status and characteristics. The
image indicates a social relationship of familial (erotic) intimacy.
The record of Israel's history as "the children of God," and then
the Christian church's formation as God's family, leaves clear in-
dicators of what the metaphor implies.

A simple exegesis beginning with Genesis 1 names the
image "male and female" in "the likeness of God," that is, the
creation of a social unit to whom God gave the command to
be a divine regent on earth. And when this account of human
genesis is expanded in Genesis 2, the writer at least grudgingly
recognizes that the full human image of God is incomplete until
woman is created. I say grudgingly because on the face of the
narrative it is clear that woman, while suitably human as a com-
panion in contrast to all the other animals, is still the partnered
servant to man, not his equal. Nevertheless she is a fully *human*
counterpart—human "flesh" and "bone"—completing the social
image. Without a partner to share his personal being Adam is
not in God's image. The story of humankind's first encounters
in social intercourse and technical achievement, which includes
recreating the image (Gen 3:1—4:2), proceeds from this point.

Adam, then, is humankind in a community relationship that excels that of a herd, a gaggle, or a swarm; and this community in its God-likeness is described in the Torah as the reflection of God's holiness. Israel as a community is admonished by Yahweh, "You shall be holy as I am holy." This "holiness" is elucidated in terms of right social relations or "righteousness." The rest of the Hebrew Scriptures give us the story of God's relationship to Israel ("the people of God") and spell out the expectations and conditions of that relationship. The image and likeness is spelled out in historical, personal-ethical terms. And it is important to point out that the narrative is *historical*, that is, the cultural specifics of the image change in the ongoing centuries. There is variation in the patterns of family and sexual relationships, but the personal-ethical character of the image remains unchanged.

Not only is God heavenly parent. The marriage metaphor is also used. God is heavenly spouse. God as Israel's husband is likened to a jealous spouse. Or God is like a pregnant woman who has given birth to children in her selfless care for them. Israel is God's firstborn (Exod 4:22; Ps 2:7). This, of course, is not unusual for the ancient imaging of God's or the gods' relation to their national following. For this reason it is important to note that the Hebrew Scriptures carefully distinguished between physical sex and sexuality as a social-relational phenomenon as we have been describing it. They are careful to avoid literalistic imaging, and practices of sacred sex in worship are strictly forbidden. In the biblical usage of these metaphors the physical aspects of sex are minimized and sexuality is understood in its personal relational sense.

While the historical biblical record of sexual regulations reflects the current cultural assumptions at the time of ancient Israel, there is a running depiction of a richer personal-social relationship mirrored in the sexual metaphor of Yahweh as husband and father to his people. This relationship moves beyond patriarchal metaphor and suggests a personal and spiritual dimension to sexuality. In spite of the inadequacy of the patriarchal metaphor, Yahweh's relation to Israel is not that of dominant male. His yearning for the intimacy of genuine relationship; his disappointment and envy when Israel is unfaithful; his gracious forgiveness that moves far beyond the limits of justice suggests the longing for the partnership of one "in his own image." And it is this sexual image that provides the social paradigm for the regulation of human sexual intimacy.

Our point here is that the image is not a spark of reason or technical intellect added to the mammalian sexual body of animal bipeds. It is rather a human image of the most intimate, even erotic, kind of social-personal and moral relationships, which suggests that the sexual orientation of humans should not be classified primarily as a physical urge or desire for genital intimacy. Nor should physical sex itself be made the ethical criterion for judging the moral character of ones sexual orientation. Human sexuality is far too nuanced and profound for such clumsy moral evaluation. While this is not the place to pursue the question of moral sexual disciplines, it must be pointed out that raising the theological significance of this metaphor also raises the moral and spiritual expectations of sexual practice.

Sexuality and the Image

The dictionary gives two definitions for the adjective "sexual." The first is a broad meaning of "related to, or associated with the sexes." The second means "having [physical] sex." In like manner "sexuality" is given a qualitative definition, and then "b. sexual activity." I begin by pointing this out because we almost instinctively think of their meaning in the opposite order. Our sex-oriented culture has led us to associate sexuality with specific physiological genital desire and behavior, and it is this reductionist view of sexuality that complicates our definition of sexual orientation and moral evaluation of same-sex relationships.

Sexuality as implied in the creation myth of Genesis 1 is an all-inclusive category characterizing our distinctly human social relationships. It is not a leftover aspect of our animal predecessors that must be strictly disciplined and inhibited. The biblical metaphor begins as a family and tribal image—an image of relationship, not a machismo individual image of male virility. It is not even the more refined image of the rational male. It is the image of male and female equality in personal erotic (sexual) relationship, which does not exclude the physical but is not defined by it. It reflects a social self-realization in relationship that we describe with the word "love" (*eros-agape-philia*). Inherent in the relationship is interdependence, mutual regard, responsibility, and pleasure in each other's presence and action—all that we include in *personal* complementarity. In short, it can be defined as an erotic relationship that finds its fulfillment in mutual creativity and enjoyment.

The conventional identification of sexuality with physical sex is a carry, over from a dualistic platonic view of humans as two distinct parts with the spirit being imprisoned in the physical. In the modern, more holistic concept of persons as psychosomatic, or in the yet more unified terms of "non-reductive physicalism," "the person is a physical organism whose complex functioning, both in society and in relation to God, gives rise to 'higher' human capacities such as morality and spirituality."[2] This nondualistic view of the human image of God seems much closer to the biblical concept than the dualism of traditional Protestant orthodoxy adapted from ancient Neoplatonism.

Human sexuality transcends the process of reproduction as it exists in even the species nearest to Homo sapiens. The personal-social and spiritual dimensions in human sexuality are integral to what Scripture describes as "the image of God." Other animals and plants also reproduce through physically sexual fertilization.

2. "Non-reductive physicalism" is the term used by Nancey Murphy of Fuller Theological Seminary for a nondualistic view of human creatures in contrast to the secularistic view of genetic determinism. She gives full recognition to the spiritual and moral (volitional) dimensions of human personhood in relationship with God. See Brown, Murphy, Malony, eds., *Whatever Happened to the Soul?*, 24.

Beyond the gradation of plants and animals, even domesticated animals, humankind was created "male and female *in the image of God*." Traditionally we have read this to mean that humans, man and wife, have been granted the honor of bearing God's image, namely, reason and volition; or that the physical sexual relationship of husband and wife expresses God's image. But it might more adequately be read that human sexuality ("male and female") transcends that of the other animals thus far created. In its personal (relational) dimension it images the divine relational pattern, which we come to understand as trinitarian.

The account makes clear that this is a sexual image by giving these god-like creatures the command to reproduce the personal-social *image*, not just a physical body. Reproduction in human sexuality is a *procreation* of the original image. After the birth of Cain and Abel and the story of Cain's fratricide, the text restates the creation of male and female in God's likeness and then adds that Adam became the father of a son, Seth, who carried on the human line "in his image" (Gen 5:1–3). In this sexual act the human family becomes, in the words of Philip Hefner, "co-creators" with God not merely mammalian stewards.[3]

The ontological status of *Adam* as human does not nullify the animal dimension of his sexuality, but it is metamorphosed like the larva into the butterfly. Human sexuality must be understood in human personal-relational terms. The image of God is not produced by mere physical fertilization of the human egg cell by a male sperm. The "co-" or "procreation" of the image is an extended physical-social project, in which the extended family of all genders is involved in its nurture. The ontological status of Adam as "co-" or "procreator" of the image of God is not merely or even primarily a physical judgment. A broader understanding of sexuality as social relationality is pivotal to evaluating the moral status and social value of the various gender orientations and individual sexual partnerships. To adapt the words of the

---

3. Hefner, *The Human Factor*, 23.

African proverb, it takes a SGLBT village to nurture the image of God in a child.

Sexuality is the morphological structure of all human social and spiritual relationships. We are physio-spiritual *persons*, whose sexual identities are located somewhere along the continuum of SGLBT, not just male and female physical bodies imbued with souls. Sexual orientation is the orientation of our personal being, the erotic dynamic that animates our social organization, and spiritual relationships. It is not only a passionate appetite of our physical bodies. Sexuality understood as the instinctual longing for human bonding and intimate physical relationships, which relations to other animals cannot provide, is an integral quality of all our relationships.

In *The Redemption of God* Isabel Carter Heyward, an Episcopal priest and teacher, states the relationship with special clarity:

> Sexuality is our experience of moving toward others: making love, making justice, in the world. It is the drive to connect; movement in love; expression of our desire to be bonded together in life and death. Sexuality is expressed not only between lovers in a personal relationship but also in the work of an artist who loves her painting; a father who loves his children; a revolutionary person who loves her people . . . And where there is no justice, no love, sexuality is perverted into violence and violation—the effects of which include rape; emotional and physical battering; relationships manipulated by control, competition, and contempt; even war itself.[4]

The "Original Image" and "Original Sin"

I have insisted that the original image of God pictured in the Genesis creation story is social and sexual. God creates (gives birth?) to creatures in his image and likeness, and humans in

4. Heyward, *Redemption of God*, 220.

turn procreate in this same image and likeness. More recently in theological discussions, especially by feminine theologians, what I have referred to as sexuality or sexual dynamic is being identified more precisely as erotic power, and defined as the psychic and emotive dynamic for all social connectedness/relatedness. It is identified with the divine dynamic that issues in creation, and reminds one of James Weldon Johnson's poem in which God looks at the world he has created, but empty of humans, and says, "I'm lonely still . . . I'll make me a man." Describing this conception of *eros* Joy R. Bostic refers to another Black author and poet of the twentieth century: "[Audre] Lorde presents the erotic as a positive central organizing force for who we are as human beings and how we relate to one another."[5]

As we have noted earlier, the erotic yearning of parent and spouse is the metaphor for God's longing to be in relationship with humankind. And the intense desire of Christian mystics for the beatific vision of God has long been pictured as the longing of earthly lovers for the consummation of conjugal desire, not as a sensory pleasure but as union with God's own self. When the erotic or sexual dynamic is understood in this more profound, comprehensive dimension rather than reduced to physical lust, then the bodily act itself is transformed into a whole pneumo-somatic (spirit-body) relationship. When the erotic is reduced to sensuous desire, its satisfaction becomes a narcissistic distortion of the creative power of love.

Laurie Jungling, in her chapter "Creation as God's Call into Erotic Embodied Relationality," characterizes God's creative *eros* as this fully embodied love: "For the purposes of this essay, I will define *eros* as the divine call into life as embodied relationality that has been freely and faithfully given in and through God's ongoing creation. Erotic love is the force that gives life the relational essence that fills and empowers all of creation."[6] This, as Jungling

5. In Kamitsuka, ed., *The Embrace of Eros*, 279. This enlarged positive understanding is foreshadowed in C. S. Lewis' *The Four Loves* (1960).

6. In ibid., 217.

indicates, emphasizes the God-like quality of *eros* as caring respect for and fidelity to the sexual partner.

The original erotic bond between husband and wife is described in this image of God, and it is this erotic power that remains at the heart of human community making. Rita Nakashima Brock puts it well in her *Journeys by Heart*: "[Original] *Eros* is a sensuous, transformative whole-making wisdom that emerges with the subjective engagement of the whole heart in relationships . . . Erotic power is the power of our primal interrelatedness. Erotic power, as it creates and connects hearts, involves the whole person in relationships of self-awareness, vulnerability, openness, and caring."[7] But we experience this original erotic grace only in its imperfect distorted forms. In creation terminology human relatedness is sexual love in its wholeness, and our original sin is the imperfect actualization of this "primal interrelatedness."

When the image is understood as love in its full embodiment, love must be defined, for it is "a many-splendored thing." It is spontaneous, passionate, desiring, free, but also relational, respectful, trusting, and faithful. The erotic especially must be understood in its personal, esthetic, and spiritual dimensions of mutual regard and honor. But sexual love in its wholeness, love that characterizes humans in the image of God, does not experience these as three separate elements that may even be in tension with each other. The image of God, especially in its trinitarian form, merges these dimensions into an organic-spiritual whole.

But, again as we noted, the original image of God as pictured in the Genesis accounts is not obvious on the face of the alienated, violent human society in which we live. If we understand original sin as sin from the very beginning (origin) of the race, as Philip Heffner suggests, we may well question whether the original image of God is not used as a literary device, not for describing an original historical human being, but as a contrasting background for describing the actual nature of our experienced

7. Brock, *Journeys by Heart*, 26.

64

human reality. It is a way of describing humanity as vulnerable, incomplete creatures as they come to clear self-consciousness, imperfect but with potentiality for fellowship and cooperation with God by virtue of creative grace. According to the accounts, the very first humans failed their first test under the most favorable circumstances! Original sin, then, is understood as the historical human reality that we experience from the beginning.

Original sin has adulterated *eros* with narcissistic desire and promiscuous freedom; and in like manner distorted *agape* into a kind of benevolence of power, and *philia* into political alliance. In the sphere of physical sexual relationships this perversion of the erotic has had dire consequences—including prostitution, rape, child abuse, adultery, and the like—which have given rise to all kinds of social malaise and physical diseases. One has only to check the thesaurus for the many synonyms describing sexual perversion to recognize the moral seriousness of the problem; for example, lascivious, lewd, lecherous, licentious, prurient, unrestrained, wanton, and many more.

Little wonder, then, that "concupiscence" became a virtual synonym for original sin in Augustinian theology. If the original sin of humanity is understood as narcissistic disposition and irresponsible action that breaks the essential connective relatedness between Creator and creature and creature to fellow creature, it is easy to understand why orthodox theology gives physical sexuality such centrality in its analysis of original sin. But care must be given not to limit original sin to its physical dimensions, and thus by implication identify the image with anatomical complementarity and reduce sexuality to physical sex.

The alienation, pride, and greed in existing humanity are not commensurate with the original image. Nevertheless, the image, flawed as it may be, remains a distinctive watermark of human uniqueness by what Nakashima Brock calls "original grace."[8] And this grace, as Leonardo Boff explains, is

8. Ibid., 135. Denis Edwards in his *How God Acts* attributes the term originally to Karl Rahner, the well-known twentieth-century Roman Catholic

not "some*thing*," but a relationship, which is the constitutive heart of human community as intended by God. In and by this graced reality the image of God becomes experienced reality in historical human community.[9]

This theological perspective on the nature of sexuality and original sin offers a significantly different perspective on the nature and moral evaluation of sexual orientation. Instead of sexual desire being attributed to an act of sin that destroyed the rational control of physical sexual relationships—as Augustine understood the Edenic situation—erotic sexual desire is viewed as good in itself, and the narcissistic perversions of it are judged as sin, both original and actual sin. Not the erotic bodily gratification and psychological ecstasy of sexual intimacy itself, but the *character of the relationship* becomes the crux. This change in the theological indictment strongly suggests a different venue for the moral evaluation of sexual orientation.

The Image in Jesus

There has been much controversy over whether and/or what Jesus had to say about sexuality, and specifically homosexuality. I am persuaded that he did speak a relevant word, and I dealt with his actual teaching in chapter 4. Here I want to point out his theological importance for a Christian understanding of the character of God in whose image humans are made, and to the theological framework in which his teachings should be interpreted. His *theological* significance is in imaging God's character as "Son of God." In 1 Corinthians 15:47–50 Paul calls Jesus "the man from heaven" in contrast to Adam "the man from the earth," and promises that we shall share his image. Colossians 1:15 calls him "the image of the invisible God," and Philippians 2:6 "the form of God." It is significant that this last reference clearly refers

theologian.

9. Boff, *Liberating Grace*. See especially chapters 3 and 4.

to Jesus as the Messianic Servant embodied in his social role, not as a theophany.

The Genesis story of creation implies that there was a paradisiacal period in Eden when the first human pair in their innocence and perfection reflected the original image. However, when Paul refers to Adam in 1 Corinthians 15:45–49 he characterizes him as the "man made of earth," with a perishable animal body in contrast to Jesus the spiritual, life-giving man from heaven (who bears the true image). As Christians understand the biblical story, it is not until Jesus, the Son of God, that the narrative presents a historical character or social archetype (the kingdom of God) perfectly in the image of God. For the New Testament writers *Jesus* is the theological model of the "original image," not the primordial Adam and Eve.

Jesus' embodiment of the Hebrew Yahweh changes the metaphor for God from emperor to servant. God is no longer perceived as an infinitely compassionate, most merciful transcendent Potentate and Judge, a view continued in Islam. God is Abba, "Immanuel"—God among us, as imaged in Jesus. This reconceptualization of the relation of Jesus to the Father leads not to a philosophical concept of the Trinity but to a trinitarian understanding of God's unity, integrity, and faithfulness as the reality to be mirrored in the human image. It is here in Jesus-as-he-relates-to-his-fellows as servant that we see the image of God.

Humans of all stripes—young and old, male and female, Jew and Gentile, tax collector or scribe, rich or poor, eunuch or father of many sons, married or unmarried, powerful or weak, straight or gay—are God's family with the real potential of participating in the family image. And whether and how they participate in that image depends in part upon whether Jesus' followers are willing to fully respect the image of God in others as they do in themselves. That is what it means to love others as they love themselves. As I have pointed out many times over the years, to be a human *person* (in God's image) is to be an "individual-in-community."[10]

Again in contrast to Islam, which also reverences Jesus as a genuine prophet of God, Jesus plays a far more radical role in challenging the traditional social order into which he was born. Indeed, his life from cradle to resurrection challenges the old social paradigm and introduces a new social construct that we refer to as the kingdom (realm, rule) of God on earth as it is in heaven. It is a construct that changes the moral and legal parameters of society, including the way in which it deals with sexuality. Traditional sexual and gender status and relationships are challenged. Family values and priorities are overturned. Sin is defined as attitudes and actions that rupture relationships, not as breaking legal and social taboos. Sinfulness is living in self-centered, hypocritical alienation. Righteousness is right relationship attained in and through the "original grace" exhibited in creation and not simply in the Law.

If this view of sexuality as the basic personal dynamic in our social relationships is a correct assessment of our situation as social-personal beings, and I believe it is, then the definition of sexual *orientation* needs to include more than deliberate attitudes and behaviors, which may be volitionally controlled. When we understand our humanity as the mutual and inseparable unity of the physical and spiritual intrinsic to each other, then sexuality cannot be attributed merely to the flesh, and sexual orientation in itself cannot be separated from the wholeness of the person, which is the inseparable union of the two.

Empirically orientation must include reflexive impulses, instinctive social behaviors, affections, genetic physical and psychological characteristics, gender perspectives, personality characteristics, and chosen personal relationships. And when we reference the theological metaphor of the image of God, it must include an erotic spirituality that is authentic to one's

10. See Kraus, *The Authentic Witness*, and Kraus, *The Community of the Spirit*.

68

psychosomatic orientation. The common line drawn by many evangelicals between orientation and "practice" or "lifestyle" becomes simply untenable. When we limit sexual orientation to physical sex attraction, which we subliminally do most of the time, we impoverish the richness of the view of sexuality implicit in the biblical metaphor of God's image.

6

An Ecclesial Response

IF THE IMAGE OF GOD IS A SOCIAL IMAGE—THAT IS, HUMAN-kind in community, rather than an individual male-female image—then the rationale for sexual regulations and an authentic contextualization of the biblical materials requires a theological reconceptualization of the moral issues involved.

How the church deals with homosexuality is a theologically ethical question, not merely a matter of moral propriety based on cultural or political aversion and literal prooftexting. The challenge is to reflect the *authentic human image of God as a community under the authority of God.* Thus the social issue of how the church deals with the inclusion or exclusion of minority sexual variants becomes a test of its authenticity as the body of Christ, the image it claims to represent in the world. It is precisely the church's claim that the spiritual reality of the image of God is attained via covenant community that gives urgency to the question of inclusion and exclusion from "the body of Christ."

Orthodoxy, as we have seen, has interpreted the image as an individual persona, and has assumed the paramount importance of morally regulating individual sexual behavior. As an unintended consequence of literal exegesis its position has often been more a reflection of conventional cultural and political values reinforced by a selective reading of the biblical text than a theological and ethical analysis and contextual application. For example, in Scripture the taboos on same-sex erotic behavior—and by implication male masturbation when it indicates an unwillingness to procreate (Gen 38:8–10)—are largely based on the divine prohibition of any ejaculation of sperm that prevents procreativity. Evangelical Protestant arguments selectively continue to enforce the sexual taboos but retract the anthropological grounds on which they are based. A theological concept of the image as God's moral character reflected in a covenanted people (sons and daughters) requires a new approach and emphasis on individual behaviors.

Sexuality is the psychosomatic basis for human social intercourse and as such is subject to social control—hopefully self-control. But what is the theological basis for such moral discipline? The moral evaluation of sexual diversity should consider the character of a person's participation in the human community, not simply his or her amorous attachment or choice. Since the image of God metaphor describes a social reality, the extent to which those of various sexual identities share in the image of God depends in part on the way in which they are included in the human community. When by social phobia and exclusion those with minority sexual orientations are treated as less than fully human—as morally damaged fragments of the image of God—the very instrument intended by God to nurture the image becomes the problem.

When the church excludes from membership those of same-sex orientation who profess faith in Christ, share its values as nonviolent Christians, and ardently persist in seeking inclusion in its discernment process because of moralistic cultural bias against erotic same-sex expressions, it denies its own spiritual genius. This is tantamount to the exclusion of Gentiles by the first generation Jewish church simply because they were uncircumcised and therefore "unclean" according to Jewish morality. In our search for the recovery of "*the new self*" and renewal "*in knowledge according to the image of its Creator*" we dare not perpetuate the scandal of Jew and Gentile, black and white, male and female, gay and straight, slave and free, citizen or illegal alien. For followers of Christ this is not a viable theological option, although it may seem to be the only political option at a given time.

The Contemporary English Version has a beautiful translation of the advice following this Colossians 3:10–11 passage just alluded to: "Christ is all that matters, and he lives in all of us. God loves you and has chosen you as his own special people. So be gentle, kind, humble, meek, and patient. Put up with each other . . . Love is more important than anything else. It is what ties everything completely together" (vv. 11b–14).[1]

At the least, theological responsibility demands that we empathetically accept such persons as participants in dialogical discernment. The church, Catholic and Protestant, has been willing to dialogue on the interpretation and application of many scriptural passages with those who differ on doctrinal and ethical issues. Increasingly the communion symbols of unity in Christ are shared with those of differing lifestyles, even in cases where there are differences on what is considered crucial doctrinal and ethical issues. But our fear and disgust on matters sexual have made it virtually impossible to mutually explore the crucial moral issues involved with our gay and lesbian brothers and sisters. What are the core values to which genuine commitment to Christ calls us? At this point a theological definition of sexual orientation becomes critical.

I have argued that sexual orientation, now understood to exist on a continuum of gender identities, should be considered an integral component in the metaphor of humans in the image of God. And that variations in sexual identity are to be accounted for as deviations in a finite order of creation, not as the morally corrupted consequences of human sin. Thus same-sex attraction in itself should not be viewed as temptation, but as a normal variant of human sexual orientation that is *subject, as are all human*

1. American Bible Society (1995).

72

conditions, to the temptations of what Paul calls "the flesh." And the definition of orientation should be understood to include the possibility of responsible sexual fulfillment under the same moral stipulations for all. If sexual identity is understood as a constituent aspect of the finite image, we have no reason to judge variant sexual orientations in themselves morally deviant.

Since the personal self-image is formed in the socialization process—which is *begun* in the biological act of conception and *realized* in responsible participation in the human community—innate sexual orientation, which is an integral part of that self-image, should be nurtured in Christian community. The challenge is to preserve the privacy and sacred intimacy of erotic ecstasy without implying that it is a shameful, clandestine pleasure, as in the Augustinian tradition; and to affirm the goodness of sexuality and sex without endorsing irresponsible indulgence, which is so widespread today. As obvious as this may seem, the Augustinian legacy, which inherently associates sexuality with illicit behavior, has made it difficult to achieve. Rather than suspicion, exclusion, and penal quarantine as moral disciplines, affirmation, inclusion, and cultivation of healthy sexual relations are required. And inasmuch as same-sex orientation is not in itself morally deviant, the requirement of celibacy becomes a legalistic impediment to church membership.

Finally, for the church, which believes that the realization of the image of God is experienced in and by participation in the "body of Christ," the ethical criterion for judging sexual behavior should not be gender orientation, but a person's commitment to and participation in the new community of the Spirit. By its own claims it has a special responsibility to nurture the renewal of the image, and in this responsibility it has its own theological grounds for understanding the spiritual and moral character of the image, which is not determined by current social and political definitions of morally acceptable sexual behavior.

"Kingdom Pragmatism:" The New Standard

Pivotal to this reappraisal of our views on sexuality, marriage, and the family is yet another messianic perspective of Jesus, namely, his insistence on the priority and urgency of the kingdom of God as the criterion for acceptance of followers. The touchstone of Jesus' ministry and teaching was clearly not the casuistic biblicism of the Pharisees with their many precisionist moral and sacramental distinctions. One might describe his reevaluation of social, moral, and religious values as *kingdom pragmatism*. His stance on nonviolence, forgiveness, and peacemaking, which took him to the cross; his clear devaluation of current family values (responsibility toward parents, and downgrading of the priorities of marriage and progeny); his acceptance of the social outcasts, diseased, despised foreigners, children, women who were victims of sexism and abuse, eunuchs, and the *hoi polloi* (generally referred to as "sinners" or "accursed") as advantaged in the kingdom of God; and his clear devaluation of the whole temple and sacramental system—all indicate a different standard of moral and spiritual evaluation.

The apostolic reevaluation of the most entrenched holiness taboos in the Jewish temple system validates this reading. Attitudes toward unclean foods, religious association with Gentiles, acceptance of eunuchs, encouragement of celibacy, putting the kingdom first, and marriage across class and religious lines ("only in the Lord") all indicate that a new standard of the image of God is in place. But the fundamental moral-spiritual virtues defining humanity in God's image—which Paul calls "the fruit of the Spirit"—remain firmly in place! These are justice, compassion, integrity, faithfulness, humility, impartiality and respect for the other person as God's image, generosity, self-denial, purity, patience, gentleness, meekness, and forgiveness (Gal 5:22–23). And again, the vices ("characteristics of the flesh") listed in the preceding verses—"fornication, impurity, licentiousness, idolatry, sorcery, enmities, strife, jealousy, anger, quarrels, dissensions, factions, envy, drunkenness, carousing, and things like that"—highlight irreligious and immoral dispositions, flaws of character, and lifestyles that persons of whatever sexual orientation are to avoid.

Apostolic patterns of adaptation to cultural diversity were a contentious issue in the early church, and it is enlightening to observe the grounds upon which adaptations were justified. Paul is the most permissive in allowing changes in the temple system's purity taboos. Indeed, the mission to the Gentiles is based on just such adaptations. He was willing to adapt on seriously debated points of religious custom considered immoral (ungodly and unclean) by the Jews, which caused serious divisions in the first-century church. In cases of institutional religious norms he offers theological rationalization for change, as in the letter to the Galatian Christians where he made a fiery argument for his changes on circumcision and associated practices, much to the dismay of his Jerusalem brothers. In other cases he freely gave advice on sexual, marital, and family matters even though he confessed that he had no direct word from the Lord. In these cases he seems to have followed a more pragmatic rule of kingdom priority.

In cases that would involve changes in the social order such as slavery, class distinctions, and women's standing and role his criterion seems to have been impartial respect for equality before God as recognized in Jesus' call into the new human community. Slaves were to be considered brothers and sisters even though they were not freed. Demeaning class distinctions were not to be recognized in the Christian community. Women were to be recognized as full fellow members in the new society established in Christ.

For this reason Paul's insistence on maintaining the practice of women's head covering in public worship comes as a surprise to moderns. In fact, he actually offers a socio-theological rationale for the practice in which he appeals to both Scripture and nature to support its practice. There is no explicit text in Paul's writings indicating a change on this point, and the women's head covering continued as an honored practice in the church for centuries in many cultures. It is only in the past century that Western churches, taking advantage of an ambiguous closing comment (v. 16), have generally abandoned the practice.

We do not know why he felt so strongly about women's head covering, although there is some evidence that women's long hair was linked with female sexuality and associated with sexual relations as well as social standing. In any case it is significant that what were considered sacred moral traditions were adapted to fit new situations, and it is important to note how they were theologically and ethically rationalized.

As with the taboo on women appearing in public shorn and/ or uncovered, Paul maintained the taboo on same-sex sexual liaisons. I observe this parallel, not to suggest that the two issues carry the same moral freight for us, but to point out the context and moral associations that were attached to such taboos. Paul undoubtedly was repulsed by "male prostitution" and "sodomy," as he indicates in 1 Corinthians 6:9–10, and he maintains the moral taboo on them. While he does not offer a theological rationale as in the case of women's head covering, judging from his pattern of contextualization it is not difficult to ascertain why Paul did not change his attitude toward homosexual behaviors. The bias against "effeminacy" in males and eunuchs in the Gentile world, the close association of homosexuality with pederasty and idol worship, the invasion of family integrity, devaluation and exploitation of women, lascivious promiscuity, and the like made it a contentious issue even in Roman society. And in the textual settings of the first chapter of Romans and 1 Corinthians 6 Paul's references are to *lifestyles rather than orientation*. The *malakoi oute arsenokoutai*, translated "male prostitutes [and] sodomites" in the NRSV, are included in lists of behaviors and lifestyles that clearly reflect the selfish, violent, idolatrous "characteristics of the flesh" that he highlights in Galatians. The question we face in making analogous moral evaluations today is whether covenanted homosexual partnerships are to be classed with male prostitution. It is at this point that the significance of the relation of sexual orientation and the image of God becomes crucial.

The example of Paul in dealing with such cases suggests that this is a question for Christian theological ethics and not for prooftexting and *ad hominem* argument. Those who claim that the very idea of sexual orientation is a homosexual stratagem "to deceive both policy makers and the public about the nature of homosexuality," as does Scott Lively, have simply defined the issues away by uncritically adopting the ancient view of the practice. They insist that homosexuality is merely an *acquired attraction* and *unnatural behavior* of innate heterosexuals. This arbitrary definitional assertion, which follows from the subliminal Augustinian assumption that equates heterosexuality with the original image, makes it possible to equate same-sex attractions with pedophilia, sadomasochism, and even bestiality.

Obviously those who are asking for inclusion in the church are not sanctioning male prostitution, pederasty, or idolatrous sacraments, so the single moral argument remaining is the traditional view of sodomy, which is thrown into question by the contemporary cultural relaxation of the taboo in heterosexual practice. If the moral taboos on oral sex, masturbation, and sodomy between men and women have been reduced to preference or taste, it is difficult to see how it can be held as the moral barrier to same-sex intimacy.

The Societal Issue

Embedded in the acceptance of sexual variety as a non-moral category is the larger and more threatening issue implied, namely, the redefinition of the role and significance of sexual intimacy in all personal and social relationships, as Jakobsen and Pellegrini note.[2] The moral and spiritual legitimacy of variety in

2. Jakobsen and Pellegrini, *Love the Sin*, 145.

sexual partnerships is an issue that the church cannot escape. Perhaps this is what is meant by the claims of the cultural right wing that political recognition of homosexual marriage threatens heterosexual marriage. But rather than becoming involved in the culture war over the political and cultural nature of homosexual marriage, the church should focus on its own theological ethical concerns in defining the parameters of sexuality.

Whether or not civil homosexual partnering is recognized for political purposes as conventional marriage, its ethical standing for purposes of the church's unique vocation needs to be *theologically* grounded. What constitutes the Christian theological-ethical base for sexual activity? Is it simply mutual consent and enjoyment, or does it necessitate a genuine love and monogamous commitment to the partner? Does the moral base require a legal recognition? Is erotic genital intimacy illicit outside of the possibility or desire for progeny? Is sexual intimacy restricted to permanent male-female relationships intended to establish a family? Answers to these questions are ineluctably involved in evaluating the morality of same-sex sexual intimacy.

All these questions except the last one apply equally to the moral discernment of both homosexual and heterosexual relations, and they frame the larger question that faces the church in our contemporary culture. For our immediate purposes, however, we need not elaborate further on these since the last question is the sticking point. *The question that vexes society and the church is whether a responsible, consensual, loving, monogamous adult sexual partnering such as morally qualifies heterosexual sexual coitus also legitimates a sexual relationship between same-sex partners.* The traditional answer to this question has been resoundingly negative based on the argument that same-sex sexual intimacy is in itself unnatural and therefore immoral.

In a predominantly heterosexual world one may well expect this negative assessment of same-sex behavior as deviant, even morally repulsive. It is not difficult to imagine situations in which heterosexuals indulging a same-sex behavior would be *ipso facto* immoral. And for a person with heterosexual identity to whom erotic same-sex sexual attraction seems weird and unnatural it is a small step from the judgment of shameful deviancy to immorality. But when two human individuals who share same-sex self-conscious identities find loving fulfillment in a covenanted partnership, it is difficult, if not impossible, to name such relationship immoral. And if it is not immoral, what grounds other than a literal reading of selected Scriptures, which has led to so many other inconsistencies of contextualization, does the church have for making it a religious requirement for membership?

Conclusion

The theological position argued in this essay levels the moral playing field and asks gay and lesbian brothers and sisters to enter the church with the same moral and spiritual expectations as the heterosexual majority. It recognizes that humans of every sexual orientation are imperfect (fallen), and that homosexual orientation is a biologically-based variant[3] in the human family made in God's image, and not a mental, physical, or moral defect. This implies recognition of same-sex erotic expression ("practice") *under the same moral rubric as that for heterosexuals: monogamous consensual covenanting relationship.*

It does not imply, as some fear, that the spiritual rationale that guided the ancient church is suddenly changed—that hedonistic promiscuity, pedophilia (or pederasty), sex experimentation, communal sex, casual sex, pornography, and prostitution are approved. It recognizes the moral and spiritual value of erotic expressions in committed same-sex relationships, but it does not

---

3. I am using the term as Carl Keener and Douglas Swartzendruber define it in their chapter in *To Continue the Dialogue*, 150. "The term *biological*, as we are using it, is an inclusive category. It includes *heredity*—our genetic makeup, the physiological processes involved in our development from a fertilized egg to an adult, and our *environment*. These are interacting components, and should be treated as part of an overall very complex system."

necessarily equate same-sex marital partnerships with hetero-sexual marriage for the purpose of procreating the race. In our society, where both church and state have a stake in marriage, each of them has freedom to address the range of political and religious issues involved. In far too many cases, the church has simply become the religious arm of the state accepting and enforcing its political and cultural mandates. May God grant us the wisdom and courage to be the community of messianic *shalom* embodying the trinitarian unity of the image of God.

PART 2

COMPLEMENTARY REFLECTIONS

7

A Pastoral Reflection

In God's Image
by Cynthia Lapp Stoltzfus

I AM GRATEFUL FOR THE CAREFUL EXPLORATION AND
thinking that Norman Kraus presents here. I respond as pastor of
a congregation that has welcomed lesbian, gay, and bisexual members for twenty-five years.[1] While our welcome has widened over
the years our definition of what it means to include LGB people
in the congregation has not stayed the same. We have variously
described this as a matter of kindness, common sense, justice,
hospitality, equality, following Jesus, and love. What we have not
consciously or publically done, in my memory, is describe our
practice as one that stems from our understanding that all people
are created in God's image.

So even though I need no convincing, it is refreshing that
Kraus looks at sexual practice and ethics through a lens other

1. My congregation, Hyattsville Mennonite Church, accepted the first
openly gay man into membership in 1986 after an extensive process of study
and prayer. Over the years we have accepted other LGB folks into membership
but thus far not any openly transgender persons.

83

than the frequently used approach of the Levitical codes. I appreciate his statement that "How we understand the metaphor of the image of God is crucial to the church's understanding of human sexuality, and vice versa." Created in the image of God, we all start on a level playing field as creatures of the Creator. All are created and called to covenant relationship with God and each other. It is this orientation toward God and neighbor and the ethical behaviors that result that should be of primary concern to the church.

Created in God's Image

Looking at the creation stories in Genesis, Micah Tillman deals with the idea of humans created in the image of God. Tillman argues that since humans are created in the image of God, our very being consists in reflecting God's presence to the world. When a human puts himself in God's place, however, the image ceases to have meaning or to even be an image. The human that has separated herself from God is not an image, but an empty mirror.[2]

It is a risk for God to create people in God's image. The human tendency is to image God rather than to find our image in God. In addition, humans tend to concretize and anthropomorphize God's image rather than focus on the action of God. To quote the late theologian Mary Daly, "Why indeed must God be a noun? Why not a verb—the most active and dynamic of all."[3] Perhaps if we reflected God's actions rather than trying to imagine God's physical characteristics our tendencies to imagine that God is like humans would be less predominant.

Being created in the image of God is complex and ambiguous. Poet John O'Donohue writes: "When the world was created,

2. Tillman teaches philosophy at Catholic University of America and is a member of my congregation. These ideas are from his presentation on Genesis during the adult education hour at University Park (MD) Church of the Brethren in January 2011.

3. Daly, *Beyond God the Father,* 33.

it was not a one-off, finished event. Creation is a huge beginning, not a finished end. Made in the image and likeness of the Divine Imagination, human creativity helps to add to creation."[4]

Creativity has come to be associated with pro-creation rather than re-creation.[5] If humanity is created in God's own image, asks Susan Brooks Thistlethwaite, "What is that image? Is it a static naturalness or is it active? Human beings are to be creative like God, and God engages humanity in the task of being stewards over all creation."[6] With O'Donohue and Brooks Thistlethwaite I affirm that part of being made in God's image is to act out the many ways that humans have been given creative power: through imagination, the arts, cultivating beauty, caring for creation.

It is this sacred creativity that is part of our image, part of who we are created to be. Is there a time when we cease being the image of God? When we hit puberty? When we are sexually active? When we are sexually active with someone of the same gender? Or is it, as Tillman maintains, when we deny that we are a reflection of the "Divine Imagination" and attempt to become the image that we reflect.

In What Image?

Mary Daly also famously wrote, "If God is male then male is God."[7] Daly's early context was the Roman Catholic Church where women are still not able to participate in the priesthood. From her perspective it looked as if the church hierarchy

---

4. O'Donohue, *Beauty*, 142.

5. The church has sometimes tied the ability to procreate with what it means to be created in the image of God. Jesus, whose sexual orientation remains a mystery, is not known to have procreated, nevertheless we hold that he was created in the image of God. This grace needs to be extended to all people who do not reproduce, or who are unable to have children.

6. Thistlethwaite, "Prop 8 Ruling."

7. Daly, *Beyond God the Father*, 19.

believed (and still practices) that only some people are created in God's image, namely, males. This allows men to hold positions of power that are declared off limits for women. Created in the image of God, males become God.

It could certainly be argued that for most of the history of Western Christian theology God has been imagined not only as male but as white. The publishing, preaching, and teaching of Christian theology and biblical interpretation was done almost exclusively by white men until the mid-twentieth century. White men held the power, made the rules, and defined the image of God.

The last half of the twentieth century brought the rise of liberation theologies and practices, along with women as pastors and teachers in seminaries. In some Christian traditions there is now a conscious attempt to loosen white male power and become anti-racist, that is, to identify institutional racism and work to eradicate it. This is ultimately an effort to understand and live out the belief that God's image is seen in *all* people, no matter their racial identity or gender. This multigenerational project demands ecclesial changes that are not easy or without pain. But it is these changes that open up the possibilities and our imaginations to understanding God in new ways.

When working for systemic change, the questions asked by people in the dominant group are important: How have sexism and racism wounded the church? How can men and white people listen, learn and change upon hearing the painful experiences of our sisters and brothers who are Latina/o, Asian, African American, African, and indigenous? How do whites and men undo the inherited privileges they still enjoy? How do we see the image of God in women and people of all races? How do we together become an honest reflection of God? How do we become the covenant community we are called to be, working together with the Spirit to bring the reign of God on earth?

Though the church has yet to finish her work of dismantling sexism and racism—stretching the imagination in terms of the image of God—the church must now also attend to heterosexism.[8] Heterosexism is tearing the church apart as straight people attempt to control theology, ethics, polity, practice, and conversation in the church. Mary Daly would not object to a paraphrase of her statement: "If God is straight, then straight is God."

The church must begin asking analogous questions about her relationship to lesbian, gay, bisexual and transgender people. How does heterosexism wound the church? How can straight people listen, learn, and change when we hear the painful stories of our lesbian, gay, bisexual, and transgender sisters and brothers and their families? What are the privileges that straight people enjoy in the church and how do we address that inequity? How can we as straight and LGBT people work together so that through the Spirit we can bring healing and hope to the world?

The Body of Christ

As Christians, the image of God becomes concrete in the body of Jesus Christ. The Apostle Paul takes the image of God one step further and tells us that the church is the body of Christ in the world. As Kraus states, "The church's challenge is to reflect the *authentic human image of God as a community under God's authority.*"

Paul carefully and extensively develops this metaphor in 1 Corinthians 12. All parts of the body are needed, even the parts that are seemingly insignificant. It is the parts that are most often reviled that are indeed essential. If, with Paul, we affirm that the body of Christ is the image of God in the world we must care for

---

8. Heterosexism is the system of unquestioned and automatic power held by heterosexuals. It assumes that all human beings have been scribed under a heterosexual template, and therefore heterosexual orientation is the only fully human option. All sexual variations are defective. Heterosexism is both personal and systemic, just as sexism and racism are present at the individual and institutional level.

that body with respect. We dare not exclude some parts because they embarrass us or we do not understand their function.[9]

The body of Christ, the image of God, is lived out differently in each congregation as each has its own charisma and gifts. Congregations that consciously include LBGT folks as part of the body receive an extra measure of spiritual gifts as well as the responsibility to utilize and respect those gifts.

My own practice includes asking how my preaching will sound to my LGB members and friends. Am I being exclusive? Is my approach to theology, discipleship, and spirituality specifically heterosexual? If the message I have is truly for everyone, gay and straight, then I must choose my words and images carefully. My assumption may be that all are created in God's image but that image is multifaceted and larger than my imagination. Keeping the LGB members in mind keeps me honest about who I think God is, how God works, and our role in the world as followers of Jesus.

Including LGB people in the congregation has meant that we have more people on whose gifts to draw for preaching, worship arts, music, and reading Scripture. The creative potential for worship is multiplied. We have adults who do not have children of their own who are eager to share their gifts in the nursery, teaching Sunday school, or with the youth. The possibilities for hospitality have widened exponentially. As we have opened our hearts and arms to LGBT people we have found ourselves opening anew to those already in the congregation as well as to refugees and asylum seekers, the homeless and people with disabilities. The body of Christ has become more complete and we have seen God in each other in new ways.

9. I have encountered those who say that gay people are a cancer that needs to be excised from the body. I would argue that this violent imagery is counter to Paul's metaphor.

Remaining Questions

Evangelical activist Ron Sider wrote in a blog post that "God loves gays, and so should we."[10] Loving is good but it is not enough. We have to take the next step and reimage God. Are we made in God's image or is God made in our image? To be the image of God in the world, to be a more inclusive body of Christ in the world, will take some rethinking, and new ways of understanding hospitality, evangelism, service, justice, and peace.

If God is seen in every person then what does it mean for the church that God is seen in LGBT people and their families? How will we read the Bible with this in mind? How will we teach children? As pastors, how will we marry and bury? How will we invite people into ministry? What in our worship practices will need to change? How will our service and witness change? And how will the church be changed by new understandings of God? These questions are not easy and may not be comfortable to ask. And yet, if we take seriously that as humans we are all created in God's image then we must ask ourselves some very difficult questions. And we will have to live into some very complex answers.

Cynthia Lapp Stoltzfus is Pastor of Hyattsville Mennonite Church in Maryland. She has studied music at Eastern Mennonite University and theology at Wesley Theological Seminary. She is married and the mother of three children.

10. Ron Sider, "God Loves Gays, and So Should We." http://blog.sojo.net/.

8

A New Testament Reflection

Born in the Image, Redeemed by the Lamb
by Mary Schertz

ETHICAL DISCERNMENT OF LIFE ISSUES HAS ALWAYS BEEN profoundly important for the body of Christ that we call the church. It has, as well, always been profoundly difficult. There are many reasons for these difficulties, but nowhere have they been more on display in recent times than in the churchly, or not so churchly, debates about homosexuality. As Norman Kraus states, "If homosexual orientation is viewed as the tragically distorted attraction of a handicapped heterosexual individual, which can and should be volitionally controlled, the cultural sanctions and social controls will take one form. If it is viewed as the self-conscious personal identity of a mentally competent, morally upright human individual who finds him/herself sexually attracted to his/her own gender, one will approach the variation in another way." To people who find themselves at one end or the other of this spectrum, the distance between these views often seems a gulf too wide to span.

For those traditions in which the biblical perspective is central, bringing the Bible into the discussion only makes the problem more complex. We come to the biblical text with different assumptions and worldviews. Those who hold a worldview that supports marriage as only appropriate between a man and a woman and assume that committed homosexual relationships are wrong will find support for their assumptions and their worldview within the text. On the other hand, those who assume that committed homosexual relationships are blessed, and whose worldview supports granting such couples the rights and responsibilities associated with heterosexual marriage, can also find support for their assumptions and worldview within the text. To be sure, the methods of argumentation tend to differ. The former often find their support in individual passages, sometimes taken out of context—literarily and culturally. The latter resort to "big picture" themes and analogies, sometimes reading carelessly and ignoring major issues of interpretation.

What Kraus does in *On Being Human* merits our careful attention because it is a rare attempt to both take careful account of what the Bible actually says and develop a broader, thematic, biblical theological perspective with integrity. In this short response, I want to appreciate the ground broken here and also test or stretch it by looking at what another major biblical theme—the cross—might add to the conversation. There is neither time nor space to do this testing fully, but I am hopeful that these short arguments can point the way toward a more genuine effort to read the Bible together on this contemporary issue; and, more importantly, to live out our disagreements in a more compassionate and more holy (thus more biblical) manner in this short piece of history we occupy. Perhaps looking at the theme similarly from a complementary perspective may have heuristic value in helping us chart the course.

Kraus suggests that in the New Testament the image of God is expanded christologically. Jesus is embodied, and in his embodiment he takes on the form or image of God. In social unity with Christ, then, believers renewed in the image of God participate in an amended reality in which "traditional religious and moral taboos and national and social identities no longer hinder the accomplishment of God's *shalom*" (p. 50). The standard of physical erotic intimacy, then, becomes not the gender of the participants in such intimacy but whether these relations mirror or distort the image of God in which we are created.

With this criterion in mind, Kraus recalls that Jesus lived out his imaging of God in ways that regularly challenged and confronted religious, cultural, and social biases, and that continue to challenge our own propensity to restrict who can participate in the "new community of the Spirit." This strongly suggests that, contrary to "casuistic biblicism," the criterion for acceptance of fellow followers rests solely on the "priority and urgency of the kingdom of God."

What I want to suggest in this brief response is that the cross of Christ is a necessary second bookend for this discussion of how the church can better engage the discernment around sexual orientation that we so desperately need. We are not only created in the image of God, but it is mirrored in the suffering love of the cross. Philippians 2:5–11 suggests that Jesus' most intense and fullest integration of his humanity—namely, his creation in the image of God and his special designation as the Son of God—is contained in his critical consent to the cross. That means many things, but at least that he integrated the divine warrior motif and the suffering servant motif present in his Hebrew Bible in such a way that he went to the cross as a non-violent divine warrior and a non-passive suffering servant. Jesus' resurrection and exaltation signify the validation of this peculiar stance chosen by Jesus when he rejected not only the sword but also the legions of angels poised to help him had he decided to choose another way. Although forgiveness is by no means new in the event of the cross, there is little doubt that Jesus' particular non-violent and non-passive response to his circumstances renewed, expanded, and activated forgiveness in a way that has been and is decisive and definitive—a necessary counterpart to our creation in God's image.

In light of this discussion of the cross I would add "and renewed by the suffering love of Christ" to Kraus's statement that
"the challenge is to reflect the authentic human image of God as
a community under the authority of God." How we deal with this
issue of minority sexual variants is a test not only of our authenticity but the authenticity of our redemption. Kraus infers that
had the Jerusalem council convened in Acts 15 come to a different conclusion about the repulsive, unholy, and uncircumcised
Gentiles, those early Christians would have denied Christianity's
own "spiritual genius." Perhaps we are at such a crux in these
times. In Acts, the Holy Spirit is active in this discernment, a
discernment that was by no means perfect. Note the many times
and various ways the issue of Gentile and Jewish relations come
up in other writings of the New Testament. It was, however, in all
its imperfection, a discernment that allowed the church to move
on together—Jew and Gentile. It was a decision characterize by
the presence of the Spirit and in the spirit of the cross of Christ.

What does the way of cross have to do with how we "covenant animals" approach this issue? I suggest that taking the way
of the cross means that we regard fellow believers as deeply human—intrinsically worthy and deeply images of God redeemed
by the blood of Jesus. I use the term "blood" deliberately, as dis-
tasteful as it is to some, because I would urge us to remember
that God somehow pulled redemption out of the gory, scandal-
ous mess of Roman crucifixion. The redemption pulled out of
scandal for human beings created in the image of God is indeed
a process of transformation. It is a process of fuller integration. It
is a process into greater love. It is a process into greater *shalom* as
we walk in the footsteps of Jesus. But it is a process rooted in the
scandal of the cross—bloody, messy, suffering love.

Kraus notes that we have erroneously understood the
image of God as a reality that pertains to us primarily as individuals. Redemption has also too often been subject to the
same erroneous limitation. We think that salvation is about
"my" receiving it and going to heaven instead of hell. That's

hardly a biblical view, let alone a New Testament view. We move toward the fullness of redemption as a body. We only find grace in relationship—relationship with God and relationship with each other. Life would be simpler, I suppose, if we could somehow be saved outside of such relationships. We are, however, partners in God's hard and holy work of saving us only insofar as we open our hearts to one another in humility and vulnerability. Does that mean that we save ourselves? As the dear Apostle would say, by no means! We can, however, make it considerably harder for God to work the transformation of redemption in our lives. Hardheartedness was not only a problem for the Israelites of the Old Testament. Hardheartedness was not only a problem the missionaries in Acts encountered. Hardheartedness remains an issue in our contemporary times and has been on full display on this issue as well as many others in the church. Nor is hardheartedness confined to any single position on an issue although we have an enormous temptation to characterize people who do not agree with us as hardhearted.

Confessing our hardheartedness and moving together into the transformation of our hearts and minds to conform to the heart and mind of Christ and be filled with the Spirit is not something we do by ourselves; and, perhaps more to the point, not something we do with the folks who agree with us. The Anabaptist traditions have many points of genius, but the tendency to divide over disagreements rather than face them is not one of them. Dividing slows the process of salvation because we need difference in order to understand and repent of our own evil. Dividing slows the process of salvation because we need difference in order to understand and move into the transformations that bring us closer to Jesus. It is not that the Spirit cannot move in groups of people who think alike. But it is, I suggest, more difficult for the Spirit to move in groups of people who think alike. Part of taking up the cross of Jesus and following after him is recognizing the role that diversity plays in our salvation. That way is the more difficult way. It is the way, however, in which we learn the transformative power of suffering love.

Does that mean that people who think homosexuality is wrong need to listen carefully to the faith stories of people who are gay, lesbian, bisexual, or transsexual? Yes. Does that mean that people who think homosexual unions acceptable and blessed by God need to attend with time and compassion to the faith stories of those who believe that receiving homosexual couples as members is wrong? Yes. Does that mean that those who find themselves somewhere else along this continuum need to listen as well? Yes. It is only by listening carefully, with soft hearts and postures of humility and prayer, that we can hope to enter into what God has for us as a body with these issues and in these times.

Taking the cross of Jesus seriously in these deliberations means taking seriously that suffering love is to be played out precisely in this arena as in all other arenas in which the church engages. When we enter the door of the church we do not choose who is there ahead of us. When we slide into the pews we do not get to choose who opens the door and comes in after us. Unlike other institutions, the church, if it indeed truly understands itself as the church and not a social club, is radically open. Unlike other institutions, which may legitimately draw similar people together, the church that only draws similar people together has ceased being the church. I once had a pastoral care professor who used to say to couples who claimed that they never disagreed, "Which one of you isn't necessary?" We need each other and, more precisely, we need people who disagree with us in order to become the people God wants us to be. That is the hard work of growing in Christ. That is the holy work of growing in Christ. That is the work of compassion that brings us close to the heart of God who loved the world to the extravagant length of sending the Son into the world that it might not perish but have life abundant.

Because we are human beings created in the image of God, because we are Christians, redeemed by the suffering love of Christ, because we are disciples growing into a greater unity with the Spirit, there can be no holier work, no more compassionate work, than to understand each other and God better by engaging these difficult debates.

Mary Schertz is Professor of New Testament at Associated Mennonite Biblical Seminary, and Director of the Institute of Mennonite Studies. She is an ordained teaching minister and a member of Assembly Mennonite Church in Goshen, Indiana.

9

A Theological Reflection

Prooftexts Are Not Enough
by Richard A. Kauffman

HOMOSEXUALITY IS ONE OF THE MOST CHALLENGING issues of our time. It is divisive of the body politic, as well as the community of faith. We should not be surprised. Our sexuality is closely tied to our identity as human beings, and for millennia most cultures have been conditioned to think only one way about the subject: heterosexual attraction and behavior is the norm, homosexual attraction or behavior is deviant—sinful, to put it in theological terms. Changes about something as intrinsic to our identity as sexuality come slowly, often in fits and starts and certainly not always in a straight, linear fashion. I remind my progressive friends of this when they grow impatient with the slow progress in the church and society towards greater inclusion of gays and lesbians.[1]

1. The seasoned historian John Lukacs says: "People do not change their minds fast. The momentum of accepted opinion and sentiments can be constrained, slow, lasting for a long time." He wasn't speaking specifically of attitudes toward homosexuality, but he might as well have been. Lukacs, *The*

Sometimes I like to imagine sitting on a perch in the future, say fifty years from now, looking back. What will the discussions and the debates we are engaged in look like from that perspective? Will the generations that come after us ask, "What was all the fuss about?" We can't be certain how these debates will turn out. And there's no getting around the contentiousness of the issues. We could wish they would go away, but the men and woman who for no fault of their own have a same-sex or bisexual orientation are not going to go away. We should not attempt to marginalize them, either by ignoring them or by scapegoating them. It is both the challenge and opportunity of our time to ask: how should a sexual minority group be regarded and treated, not least of all in the "company of the committed," the church?

To deal with this issue head on, we need daring, thoughtful people who will not flinch from the subject, who will muster their best intellectual and intuitive gifts to help us think in ways that we have not thought heretofore. That is what I believe C. Norman Kraus is attempting to do in *On Being Human*. And for that the church owes him a debt of gratitude. What he asserts here is not all that can be said, and it is certainly not the final word. But it is a helpful word for our times, for both church and world as they wrestle with the place of men and woman who happen to have same-sex attractions, many of whom would like to be in covenanted relationships on par with those of us who are married to persons of the opposite sex.

Kraus and I agree on at least two fundamental points: one, that there is something like a same-sex attraction, what some would call "constitutional homosexuality," that is a given and not a choice. Indeed, homosexuality as we've come to understand it has three dimensions: attraction, identity, and activity. Gays and lesbians are *attracted* sexually to persons of the same sex. In time many of them come to have a homosexual *identity*: "This is who I am," they claim. And some, not all, *act out* their attraction in sexual relationships with other persons of their own gender.

Future of History, 50.

This relatively new awareness of constitutional homosexuality raises the inevitable questions then: If it is not a choice, how can they be blamed for their orientation? And if it is not a choice, then what are they to do with their attraction? Should they be given the freedom to enter into relationships with a person of the same sex that is the equivalent of traditional marriage? Or should they adhere to the traditional Christian understanding of marriage and sexual conduct—that marriage is between a man and a woman who enter into a lifelong covenantal relationship, while sexual activity is proscribed outside such heterosexual relationships? Celibacy for persons with a same-sex attraction is the logical conclusion for those who would stick to a strict traditionalist perspective. It is against this restrictive position that Kraus mounts an argument for granting permission to homosexual persons to enter into relationships with persons of the same-sex on the same terms as heterosexuals: lifelong, monogamous, covenantal relationships.

Second, Kraus and I appear to agree on another matter: that the Bible is our ultimate authority in matters related to how we should live as disciples of Christ, but that the particular texts that speak to homosexual activity are not necessarily definitive for our times. This latter assertion is a consequence of studying those half dozen or so texts in their context and realizing that the way they apply to our own context is at best quite ambiguous. Christians disagree as to their meanings, if not in their original context, then in how they should apply to our context some two millennia and more later. To find scriptural guidance for how we should confront this new awareness of constitutional homosexuality, we should look to broader themes of Scripture and to trajectories within Scripture that may take us beyond the scriptural horizons themselves.

The appropriate Christian instinct when faced with new dilemmas is to look for wisdom and guidance from the Scriptures. As someone has noted, each new present has within it the possibility of a new past. Challenged by new data and experience, we return to Scripture and, not surprisingly, discover new insight. As the Puritan leader John Robinson noted, "The Lord hath more truth and light yet to break forth from His holy Word." Biblical revelation suggests trajectories that have led the church in subsequent centuries to adopt positions that the Bible itself did not explicitly sanction, such as the ordination of women—new truth and light, indeed.

The church has a justifiable impulse to explore how the church in times past has dealt with comparable issues. Indeed, on that the Bible itself provides some examples. One early challenge to the church was whether Gentile believers needed to become Jewish in order to be fully Christian. That is, must male Gentile believers be subjected to circumcision? A council in Jerusalem aired out the issues and a way forward was reached that appeared to be a Holy Spirit-led resolution (Acts 15). Yet we know that the issue wasn't settled forever and a day. It continued to be an issue within the apostolic church.

Another example closer to our time took place during the antebellum era in the United States in the struggle to abolish slavery. This provides a case study not unlike the current battles in the church over the Bible on homosexuality. Some Christians had made up their minds what they believed about slavery: knowing in their hearts and minds that slavery was wrong, they didn't really care what the Bible had to say, at least not on this issue. A quite opposite group, what we would call the literalists, took the Bible very seriously. They realized that in much of the Bible slavery is assumed and there doesn't seem to be an explicit condemnation of it. It is not too much of a stretch to say that the literalists had the best prooftexts on their side, which, of course, was what they were looking for. A third group realized that the issue of slavery could not finally be decided on the basis of scriptural texts that dealt explicitly with the institution or practice of slavery. Rather, the issue had to be discerned by more considered discernment of broader themes in Scripture about what it means to be created in the image of God and of Scripture's own trajectory toward the negation of boundaries between Jews and Gentiles, free and slave, men and women since all are now one in Christ.[2]

This seems to be where the church is today on homosexuality: one faction knows what they think and believe about gays and lesbians and they don't care what the Bible or the church has to say about it; another holds to a literal interpretation of a narrow range of scriptures that speak of homosexual acts without an awareness of a constitutional homosexuality; and finally, some are convinced that more sophisticated theological reflection is needed that takes into account broader themes of Scripture and new light from our contemporary context including insight drawn from both human and natural sciences. I place Kraus in this latter category.

Kraus does not engage much in a project of deconstruction of discrete Scripture texts on homosexuality. However, he does engage in the deconstruction of a particular theological tradition—a tradition that begins with Augustine, but continues to echo through evangelical readings of Scripture on sexuality, including particularly homosexuality. Most of Kraus's attention is focused, however, on a constructive theological project, utilizing sustained reflection on the biblical teaching on the image of God, rooted in an implicit trinitarian theology and culminating in an authentic community of messianic *shalom*. Same-sex relationships should not be seen as deviant, but rather "a normal variant of human sexual orientation that is *subject as all human conditions to the temptations of what Paul calls 'the flesh.'*" Responsible sexual conduct for homosexuals therefore should be subject to the same standards expected of heterosexuals. The exclusion or inclusion of gays and lesbians is tantamount to the rejection or acceptance of Gentiles by the early church because Gentile male believers weren't circumcised and therefore were considered unholy and unclean by Jews. From Kraus's perspective, then,

2. See Noll, *The Civil War,* and Noll, *God and Race in American Politics.*

persons with a same-sex attraction provide an ultimate test for the church of whether it is indeed a community of the Spirit.

It is not my role here to recount the case that Kraus makes for inclusion of persons with same-sex attraction and commitments. Readers can digest that for themselves. My role here is to give some response. Hence, I would like to suggest that Kraus might be helped hermeneutically by employing the so-called Wesleyan Quadrilateral. Borrowed though it might be for persons from the Anabaptist tradition, it is a useful tool for theological reflection on a subject such as homosexuality.[3] Going beyond the Protestant notion that Scripture alone is authoritative in matters of faith and life, the Wesleyan Quadrilateral makes more explicit what is often assumed: that there are other sources of truth besides biblical revelation—tradition, reason, and experience. I suggest this as a complement to Kraus as I think that if he had consciously drawn on such a view of authority, he would have had more to say about two areas: reason and experience. In the Wesleyan Quadrilateral reason is the category under which human knowledge such as science is considered. Kraus might have engaged in more extended dialogue with scientific studies, particularly genetics, and related causation with respect to homosexuality. Engagement with research on this front would strengthen Kraus's case that homosexuality for most persons is not a choice but rather a given.

Further, Kraus might have had more to say about how experience shapes our attitudes, perceptions, and convictions on homosexuality. He more or less assumes the experience of homosexuals, but we don't hear much about their actual experiences: coming to an awareness that they are different from the dominant sexual group, in many cases coming out, in some cases entering into covenantal relationships, but mostly not getting the support needed from church or society for what is needed

3. I have more to say about my own discovery of the Wesleyan Quadrilateral in the autobiographical essay, "Beyond Criticism: My Life with the Bible," in Gingerich and Zimmerman, *Telling Our Stories*, 121–34.

to nurture long-term, faithful relationships. Again, Kraus does not deny this reality; he more or less assumes it. But if experience is part of the datum of theological reflection, one might have wished for him to take on the lived reality of homosexuals more self-consciously.

Experience also raises the question as to how people reach conclusions on this vexing issue or how their opinions and perspectives change in time. Do people think their way through such an issue? Or does experience and intuition lead them toward tentative conclusions on which they must then build their own rationale? How was it for Kraus? It may well be that he has largely thought his way into and through this issue. But I suspect there is a story to be told here as well, and perhaps the reader would benefit from having such disclosure. In any case, my experience with most people is that they are more or less forced to rethink their preconceptions about homosexuality through discovering that someone they know quite well is gay or lesbian.

There is another aspect of experience relative to homosexuality that is little talked about, what some people call the "yuck factor" (Kraus does recognize this reality several times). Let me offer a confession: I must admit that I am hopelessly and helplessly heterosexual. This has several implications: I don't remember a time when I didn't have heterosexual impulses. Truth be told, some of my earliest childhood memories involve sexual attraction to women. My sexual orientation has never been a matter of willful choice. I am heterosexual; it is what it is and I really haven't had a choice in the matter. In fact, it is part of my identity, who I am as a human being. I don't know what it is like to be gay or to have a same-sex attraction. As a Christian empowered to bear others' burdens, I should make a good-faith effort to learn from gays about their experience, not least of all their experience of being marginalized in a heterosexually dominant culture. Before criticizing someone's experience, I should at least attempt to understand it. For that I need to hear their stories, learn about their experience. But here is the point I really want to make. When I first heard about (male) homosexuality many years ago, my internal response was, "They do *what* with each other? Yuck. How gross is that?!" Such a response today would be appropriately called homophobic. But let's be honest: this is a major reason why progress is slow toward empathetically understanding people with a same-sex orientation. I have a friend who is a pastor of a congregation that has come to a position of identifying itself as a welcoming and affirming congregation. To reach that point, she told me, they had to explicitly talk about this "yuck factor," which was largely a response from male heterosexuals toward male homosexuals.[4]

Experience as an element in theological reflection is not intended to be only about personal experience. It entails the experience of groups, not least the church in its various forms (congregational, denominational, ecumenical). And experience cannot be the final norm. But experience certainly provides the grist for ongoing theological reflection, even as it was a crucial element in the formation of Scripture itself and the development of church tradition.

In conclusion, I'd like to ask several questions. These questions are directed as much toward the church as it struggles with issues related to same-sex orientation as they are toward Kraus.

1. Does this contentious issue need to be a church-dividing issue? On this question I speak out of my own personal experience. Two years ago my church had a major crisis over this issue. A lesbian couple attending our congregation seemed to be accepted well until the issue of membership was raised. Then the congregation quickly polarized over the issue, and we lost about a third of our people, including the lesbian couple. Since then the congregation has engaged in a process of healing and discernment. While we have not yet reached a resolution, we are reaching toward a position that answers this question in the negative: no, it doesn't have

4. Nussbaum argues this yuck factor is skillfully used politically in the culture wars in Nussbaum, *From Disgust to Humanity*.

to be a church-dividing issue. In the meantime, we have determined that this issue raises another question for us, namely, how can we be church with each other in the midst of this contentious issue? We are seeking a resolution that not only respects the opinions of people on both sides of this issue, but that also embodies both sides. It is too soon to say whether we will reach such a conclusion.

2. If we are to move in the direction Kraus suggests, then what will the teaching position of the church be toward sexuality in general and marriage in particular? What do we teach our children and young people about sexuality, who often have confusing ideas about sex, not least of all about their own sexual identity? Also, it appears as though Kraus does not want to change the traditional definition of marriage, while at the same time allowing persons of same-sex orientation to enter into comparable relationships with each other. If not marriage, then just what is the nature of these same-sex relationships? What are we to say about same-sex couples having and raising families? And should not the church in some way put its blessing on these relationships, calling same-sex couples to covenant relationships with the same expectations as the church holds for heterosexual couples? Kraus does suggest that the church should regulate homosexual behavior, but he doesn't have much to say about what that looks like or how it should be done. I agree with William Stacy Johnson that it is theologically irresponsible for the church to welcome and affirm gays without also ordering their relationships. What is also needed is some kind of act of consecration that takes place within the context of the covenanted community.[5]

The sad reality about the church's preoccupation with homosexuality is that heterosexuality receives very little discussion.

---

5. Johnson, *A Time to Embrace*, 95 ff. See also Rogers Jr., "Sanctified Unions"; Rogers Jr., "Same-Sex Complementarity."

For most of us, in these debates about homosexuality we're mostly talking about someone else's sexuality. We should not feel comfortable talking about someone else's sexuality if we're not willing to talk about our own. Perhaps what we need is a slight but significant change of subject: could we talk instead about what we expect of each other—regardless of sexual orientation—with respect to how we conduct ourselves as sexual beings? To what standards should we be holding one another? That could be a fruitful conversation, if we dare to engage it.

Richard A. Kauffman, Glen Ellyn, Illinois, is a senior editor of *The Christian Century*, and a member of Lombard Mennonite Church. Prior positions include congregational pastoring, editing for Herald Press, seminary administration, and teaching in theology.

10

Author's Epilogue

WHEN I BEGAN THIS WRITING PROJECT I HAD NO INTEN-
tion of publication. I realized that over the past quarter century
I had changed my mind considerably on the subject of sexuality,
and while I had studied the biblical teachings, much of my theological change had been intuitive, based on my experience in the
church and expanded knowledge of the subject. I realized that I
was reading the biblical materials from a different anthropological and theological perspective, and needed to study more closely
the theological tradition in which the moral position of the evangelical church is rooted. The different exegetical interpretations of
discrete biblical passages were based on different theological and
cultural perspectives and assumptions. I needed to examine more
closely why experience had changed my intuitive approach to the
subject. Thus my analysis of the theological and cultural tradition
rather than a reexamination of individual biblical texts.

In my essay I have focused on the church's need for a theologically based ethics of sexuality in contrast to a socio-politically
based ethics. But what is included in "theology"? The answers to
that question are spoken to in the above reflections of a pastor,
a New Testament scholar, and a theologically trained editor of
an ecumenical church periodical. Cynthia Lapp, the pastor of an
inclusive congregation, puts the theological challenge in concrete

language: "How do we [as a congregation] together become the honest reflection of God? . . . Keeping the LBG members in mind [when I preach] keeps me honest about who I think God is." Mary Schertz, a professor of New Testament, asks, "What does the way of cross have to do with how we 'covenant animals' approach this issue?" And she reminds us that the church's concept of salvation is at issue in the way we respond to matters such as this one that affects our agapeic respect for and relation to others.

Christian theology, as Richard Kauffman reminds us, must include the experience of Christians, not least in the way we do church, and the use of our rational faculties in the cultural framing of biblical insight. Theology is not a dogmatic text with all the answers. It is a very personal process of discovery in which one constantly seeks to understand the implications of Jesus Christ for the ever-changing cultural kaleidoscope. For this purpose the church needs not only to exegete the biblical text, but also to correctly exegete the current cultures in which it is embedded. As historians remind us, it is the changing present that necessitates the rewriting of past history, not to change its realities, but to utilize its wisdom.

The present monograph is not a theological polemic attempting to analyze and dissect the stereotyped arguments for and against acceptance of sexual deviation. But, as Kauffman points out, I do try to examine and deconstruct the theological culture that has provided the framework, assumptions, and vocabulary for the debate that is rocking the church. It is my conviction that we must reframe the issues in order to reconstruct a Christian ethic that reflects the character of God as seen in the life of Jesus. Or to use a figure from my colleague Howard Zehr, we must "change our lenses," which after long use no longer help our aging eyes focus on the original biblical message of God's creative love. We must examine critically the subliminal theological custom of identifying God's essential being with sexual gender. For, as Cynthia, alluding to Mary Daly, challenges us, "If God is strait, then strait is God."

In pressing the issue as a theological one for the church I am really raising the question whether our different views on the nature of sexuality should be considered matters of closed *dogmatic* certainty or open to continuing discernment both scientifically and theologically. There is little likelihood there will be anything like unanimity on the issues in the coming decades, and the question is whether this is a matter for summary exclusion of those in disagreement with "orthodox" views, or a matter for continuing exploration and discernment. If it is the latter, then the intrachurch conversation needs to include committed believers of all sexual identities at the table. We must, as Kauffman suggests, arrive at a position that "not only respects but embodies both sides."

In the spirit of Rowan Williams, Archbishop of Canterbury, for whom the issue has been agonizingly existential, in this as in many moral decisions the question is "How can we so act as to *show* the character of God?" And as Mike Higton observes, "[This] is a question which demands of us not just knowledge (of what the law demands) but *wisdom*: the kind of responsiveness, discrimination and insight built up by slow, deep learning of the nature of God."[1]

---

1. Higton, *Difficult Gospel*, 135.

Bibliography

Boff, Leonardo. *Liberating Grace*. Maryknoll, NY Orbis, 1981.

Bostic, Joy R. "'Flesh that Dances': A Theology of Sexuality and the Spirit in Toni Morrison's *Beloved*." In *The Embrace of Eros: Bodies, Desires, and Sexuality in Christianity*, edited by Margaret D. Kamitsuka, 277–97. Minneapolis: Fortress, 2010.

Brock, Rita Nakashima. *Journeys by Heart: A Christology of Erotic Power*. New York: Crossroads, 1994.

Brown, Warren S., Nancy Murphy, and Newton Malony, eds. *Whatever Happened to the Soul?: Scientific and Theological Portraits of Human Nature*. Theology and the Sciences. Minneapolis: Fortress, 1998.

Collins, Kenneth. *Exploring Christian Spirituality*. Grand Rapids: Baker, 2000.

Daly, Mary. *Beyond God the Father: Toward a Philosophy of Women's Liberation*. Boston: Beacon, 1973.

Edwards, Denis. *How God Acts: Creation, Redemption, and Special Divine Action*. Theology and the Sciences. Minnesota: Fortress, 2010.

Finger, Thomas. *Self, Earth and Society: Alienation and Trinitarian Transformation*. Downers Grove, IL: InterVarsity, 1997.

Foucault, Michael. *The History of Sexuality: An Introduction*. New York: Random House, 1990.

Gagnon, Robert. *The Bible and Homosexual Practice*. Nashville: Abingdon, 2001.

Gingerich, Ray and Earl Zimmerman, eds. *Telling Our Stories: Personal Accounts of Engagement with Scripture*. Telford, PA: Cascadia, 2006.

Hauerwas, Stanley, and William H. Willimon. *Resident Aliens: A Provocative Christian Assessment of Culture and Ministry for People Who Know That Something Is Wrong*. Nashville: Abingdon, 1989.

Hefner, Philip. *The Human Factor: Evolution, Culture, and Religion*. Minneapolis: Fortress, 1993.

Heyward, Isabel Carter. *The Redemption of God: A Theology of Mutual Relations*. Lanham, MD: University Press of America, 1982.

Higton, Mike. *Difficult Gospel: The Theology of Rowan Williams*. New York: Church, 2004.

Bibliography

Hubbard, Ruth, and Elijah Wald. *Exploding the Gene Myth.* Boston: Beacon, 1993.

Hunter, James Davidson. *Culture Wars: The Struggle to Define America.* New York: Basic Books, 1991.

Jakobsen, Janet R., and Ann Pellegrini. *Love the Sin: Sexual Regulation and the Limits of Religious Tolerance.* New York: New York University Press, 2003.

Johnson, William Stacey. *A Time to Embrace: Same-Gender Relationships in Religion, Law, and Politics.* Grand Rapids: Eerdmans, 2006.

Kamitsujka, Margaret D., ed. *The Embrace of Eros: Bodies, Desires, and Sexuality in Christianity.* Minneapolis: Fortress, 2010.

Khouj, Abdullah Muhammad. *Islam: Its Meaning, Objectives, and Legislative System.* USA: Khouj, 1974.

Kraus, C. Norman. *The Authentic Witness.* 1979. Reprint. Eugene, OR: Wipf & Stock, 2010.

———. *The Community of the Spirit,* Scottdale, PA: Herald, 1993.

———. *To Continue the Dialogue: Biblical Interpretation and Homosexuality.* Telford, PA: Cascadia, 2001.

———. *God Our Savior: Theology in a Christological Mode.* Scottdale, PA: Herald, 1991.

La Cugna, Catherine Mowry. "The Practical Trinity." In *Exploring Christian Spirituality,* edited by Kenneth J. Collins, 273–82. Grand Rapids: Baker, 2000.

Lewis, C. S. *The Four Loves.* New York: Harcourt Brace Jovanovich, 1960.

Lukacs, John. *The Future of History.* New Haven, CT: Yale University Press, 2011.

Milgrom, Jacob. *Leviticus: A New Translation with Introduction and Commentary.* Anchor Bible 3A. New York: Doubleday, 2000.

Noll, Mark A. *The Civil War as a Theological Crisis.* Chapel Hill, NC: University of North Carolina Press, 2006.

———. *God and Race in American Politics: A Short History.* Princeton, NJ: Princeton University Press, 2010.

Nussbaum, Martha C. *From Disgust to Humanity: Sexual Orientation & Constitutional Law.* New York: Oxford University Press, 2010.

O'Donohue, John. *Beauty: The Invisible Embrace.* New York: HarperCollins, 2004.

Pronk, Pim. *Against Nature: Types of Moral Argumentation Regarding Homosexuality.* Grand Rapids: Eerdmans, 1993.

Rogers Jr., Eugene F. "Same-Sex Complementarity: A Theology of Marriage." *The Christian Century,* May 11, 2011.

———. "Sanctified Unions: An Argument for Gay Marriage." *The Christian Century,* June 15, 2004.

Socarides, Charles. "The Sexual Deviations and the Diagnostic Manual." *American Journal of Psychotherapy* 32 (1978) 414–26.

Swenson, Eric. "Becoming Myself: A Transgender Pastor's Story." *The Christian Century,* March 9, 2010, 28–33.

Bibliography

Thistlethwaite, Susan Brooks. *Adam, Eve, and the Genome: The Human Genome Project and Theology.* Theology and the Sciences. Minneapolis: Fortress, 2003.

———. "Prop 8 Ruling: Nothing 'Wrong' with Being Gay." *Washington Post,* On Faith, August 9, 2010.

Tickle, Phyllis. *The Great Emergence: How Christianity Is Changing and Why.* Grand Rapids: Baker, 2008.

Tillich, Paul. *Systematic Theology.* Vol. 2: *Existence and the Christ.* Chicago: Chicago University Press, 1957.

Wiley, Tatha. "*Humanae vitae,* Sexual Ethics, and the Roman Catholic Church." In *The Embrace of Eros: Bodies, Desires, and Sexuality in Christianity,* edited by Margaret D. Kamitsuka, 99–114. Minneapolis: Fortress, 2010.